CONTENTS

CONTENTS

INTRODUCTION

A brief conversation prompted the writing of this book.

"I'm selling my house." reported a friend. Then after some thought she added, "Well, when I say I'm selling my house, what I mean is I've instructed estate agents to sell it."

"Oh," says I, "do they seem like good salesmen?"

"Salesmen?" came the incredulous reply, "they're not salesmen, they're estate agents."

"Ah," says I, not wishing to repeat myself, "so if they're not selling it, and you're not selling it, who is exactly?"

"Good point."

And the point is this – to sell a property it must be presented and promoted as a desirable article, not plonked on the market with a hope and a prayer. Whether the services of estate agents are used or the property is advertised privately, there is still the need to compete favourably with other properties to have any hope of finding a buyer. With hundreds of smart new houses and flats being built each year, anyone trying to sell their home is in direct competition with some of the biggest names in the property business. These people have researched the British public well, and really know what they are doing when it comes to tempting buyers. Can you say the same?

In a depressed housing market, selling property becomes a challenge few of us embark upon lightly. What are the chances of getting a good price, we ask ourselves? Will the family stand the strain? Are all estate agents negotiators from hell? Is it really worth the bother?

But fear not. This book sets out to help by showing how to actively sell property. From getting the most out of estate agents, to turning casual applicants into eager buyers. From recognising tricks of the trade used by house builders, to learning skills for successful selling. So, if you are determined to find a buyer quickly and get the best price, read on.

FOR PURPOSES OF SIMPLICITY, IT HAS BEEN ASSUMED THAT READERS WILL USE ESTATE AGENTS AND SOLICITORS. HOWEVER, THE PRINCIPLES APPLY EQUALLY TO PRIVATE VENDORS AND THOSE WHO DO THEIR OWN CONVEYANCING.
ALSO FOR SIMPLICITY, AND TO AVOID THE TIRESOME USE OF 'HE OR SHE', THE MASCULINE TERM HAS BEEN USED THROUGHOUT.

ESTATE AGENTS

The majority of people use estate agents when selling their home, believing this is the only way to do it. It isn't. Most local newspapers deal with private property advertisements and several books are available on the subject of selling without agents. In this chapter we look at the way estate agents operate, what can be gained from using their services and how to get value from their considerable fees. After reading it you should be in a better position to decide whether or not using an estate agent is right for you. For those who have already decided to go it alone, I salute your bravery, wish you the best of luck and suggest you turn to the next chapter.

How estate agents work

They will defend to the death their self-styled image as sales executives, but the involvement of most estate agents in actually "selling" a property is limited, in that their work centres mainly on promotions to attract applicants and often stops short of turning those applicants into buyers. In short, the property is placed with an agent at the agreed price and written details are compiled. These details are then sent to people who request them (referred to as applicants) as a result of advertising through the media, telephone canvassing, mail shots and For Sale boards. Viewing appointments are then arranged for interested applicants, and when an offer is accepted the tricky stuff is handed over to solicitors and finance bodies. That's it.

That is not to say that estate agents are irrelevant to the property market, but the job of actually selling a property usually lies squarely with the owner, and the amount of effort put into the process will often dictate how quickly a buyer is found. Estate agents play an important role in keeping the market active, but their services are geared more towards buyers than sellers (or vendors, as they are known).

Their advertising and distribution value is obvious, but it is a mistake to assume they are all blessed with sales skills. Careful selection of your agent helps, but the vendor who hands over the entire job of selling to an agent is likely to be disappointed.

> **TOP TIP**
> Do not underestimate the importance of estate agents
> as promotion tools. It is vital to instruct agents
> who are adept at marketing
> and advertising.

Once an offer has been accepted, some exceptional agents prove themselves invaluable as mediators between buyer and vendor, keeping things running smoothly right up to completion. Sadly many don't bother, being of the opinion that their job is over once an offer has been received, and vendors need to look hard to find the rare breed of agents who do return telephone calls and know more about the property market than they know about endowment policies and life insurance.

Although there are recognised estate agency qualifications, it is not an operational requirement for agents to hold such qualifications. Potential members of the National Association of Estate Agents (NAEA) do not need a pocket full of certificates to join, but a satisfactory performance at a verbal interview is required before membership is granted. Since the NAEA sets standards of practice, vendors may wish to find out which agencies are members because this is the only formal assessment most of them have. Having said that, a professional qualification is not the only thing you should be looking for in a good agent: natural dynamism to achieve in such a competitive field is what really counts. Above all, your agent needs experience, enthusiasm and a flair for dealing with people.

Choosing your agent

Before inviting any agents to value your property, it is a good idea to scrutinise the local newspaper. From this you will be able to see:

- which agents advertise heavily; and
- the market each agent is aiming at.

Different agents cater for different areas of the property market, so it is far better to place your instructions with an agent who is used to dealing with your type of property. For example, not all agents are experienced with land sales, so a property with acreage should be marketed through an agent who specialises in this field (excuse the pun!).

When you have selected a list of agents, telephone them or visit their office. Ask what services they offer to clients and let them sell themselves to you. If they can't, strike them off the list. If they are unable to sell their own services you can assume they have no confidence in their ability and little enthusiasm for the job.

When you have narrowed the choice of suitable agents down, slim it still further by taking a close look at each office.

- Is it in a good position for passing trade?
- It is clearly visible to prospective buyers looking for an agency?
- Are property details displayed in the window, and are they clear and attractive?
- Do the staff appear professional?
    - are they answering the telephones promptly?
    - are they quick to offer assistance, or do they leave you to wander around aimlessly?
- Does the office seem efficient and, most of all, busy?
- Is the office open long hours and weekends?

Also, observe the way administration is dealt with – are the desks tidy and enquiries dealt with in an organised manner, or are the staff fumbling around in total chaos? If so, re-think. You need a competent administration system which handles enquiries efficiently and quickly. You do not want to find out later that keen applicants slip through the net because of inept office systems.

TOP TIP

Watch the way you are treated by agency staff to get a good idea of how prospective buyers of your property will be dealt with.

Lastly, find out as much as possible about the background of the company or partnership. Ask how many (if any) of the staff are NAEA members, to see if they are a professional team or just a mixed bag of office workers filling in time between other jobs. The length of time an agency has been in business gives an indication of its success rate, and you could also ask about their sales record for that year. You might not get the whole truth, but at least you will portray yourself as one who knows a thing or two about property, and not someone to be fed a line.

DID YOU KNOW? *In Scotland solicitors have traditionally acted as selling agents, so vendors north of the border have the choice between using estate agents or the various solicitor-based marketing services such as Solicitors' Property Centres, Solicitors' Estate Agencies and Solicitors' Property Registers.*

Independents or nationals?

The property boom of the 1980s not only saw a huge growth in the number of independent estate agencies in the high street, but also opened the way for some banks, building societies and other finance sector companies to get in on the act. Some of the large estate agency chains now come under the banner of institutions previously more concerned with funding the purchase of property than selling it. As a result, some of the small independent agencies have been squeezed out by such daunting competition. This is tragic for them, but helpful to the vendor in weeding out the weak from the strong, since in this dog-eat-dog marketplace only the fittest have survived.

When commenting on the working practices of national and independent agencies, it would be unfair to suggest that one is more successful or capable than the other. However, they do operate differently so, as a general observation only, the differences of each can be summed up as follows:

	Independents	Nationals
Nation-wide representation		✓
Aggressive sales techniques		✓
Extensive advertising	✓	✓
Prominent High Street position	✓	✓
Experienced staff	✓	✓
Customer care and attention	✓	
More colour photography used in written details	✓	
Flexibility	✓	
Local knowledge	✓	✓

Of course not all independent agents are flexible in their approach to clients and not all national agents have aggressive staff, so the vendor will need to decide which particular agency impresses him.

The biggest advantage for choosing a national agency from a promotional point of view is that a company which has offices up and down the country has access to potential buyers in neighbouring areas as well as the vendor's local town, which is especially useful when the property is located midway between two towns. However, some independent agencies are more successful than their national competitors despite this, so wider representation is not the only aspect to consider.

Independent agencies are invariably run and managed by the owner (or partners) of the company, which tends to mean they instil in their staff the importance of a good reputation and are usually at pains to develop and maintain good client relations.

Sole or multiple agency?

On the surface, the only difference between placing your property with one agent on a sole agency agreement, or instructing several agencies under multiple agency agreements, is the commission fee your agent(s) will charge, since this will almost certainly be higher if you opt for the latter. You must decide whether greater saturation is worth a higher fee, but where for example all the estate agencies are sited near one another, it may not be necessary to enlist more than one agency because potential buyers will probably register with all the offices in the town anyway.

If your intention is to instruct more than one agent with the aim of greater exposure, consider carefully both the advantages and disadvantages of market saturation. If your property is likely to secure a quick sale (usually the only guarantee of which is a very keen price) but you want to be absolutely sure of maximum exposure, saturating the market might be a good idea, enabling you to reach all applicants registered with all suitable agents at the time the property is marketed. In theory, casting the net wide enough gets a good catch. However, it is worth bearing in mind that if the saturation ploy doesn't work, you have exhausted the prospect of securing a new promotion by switching agents because there will be none left who have not had a go at selling the property, which will have become 'stale' from over exposure.

To confuse the choice between sole and multiple agency arrangements still further, there is another factor to consider and that is the enthusiasm (or lack of it) which agents will muster to secure a sale, depending on the type of agreement they are working under. With a sole agency agreement, complacency could be a problem. The agent does not have any competition, so there is a tendency to behave as if the property is on the books for as long as it takes to sell. On the other hand, with a multiple agency agreement, agents may be less inclined to spend a lot of time and money marketing a property if they fear another agency might sell it first.

DID YOU KNOW? *It is not permissible for a vendor to have more than one For Sale board on his property.*

In some cases, as a compromise between sole and multiple agency arrangements, two agents work together on a split-commission basis. Both agents market the property in the usual way, then split the fee between them, regardless of which one finds the buyer. This works best with agencies who have a good relationship with one another.

Evaluating the selling price

At the vendor's invitation the agents will visit the property primarily to give their opinion of its market value (or what they think they can sell it for), but before inviting any agents to give a valuation the vendor should already have a good idea of what the property is worth. The best way to do this is by researching similar properties for sale in the area to ascertain the going rate. Be watchful though, of optimistically valued properties which have been on the market for a long time. It may suit the owners of these properties to wait indefinitely to achieve a high price, but it is not a realistic reflection of market values.

DID YOU KNOW? *As a result of financial collapse in the housing sector after the 1980s property boom, thousands of home owners found the value of their homes had dropped considerably. A survey in 1993 reported that 27% of homes bought between 1987 and 1991 were worth less than the mortgage on them. This disturbing trend is known as* negative equity.

Get at least three valuations from different estate agents, but don't be tempted necessarily to instruct the one who values highest. Agents are wise to the fact that homeowners have a tendency to do this, so they sometimes value high just to get the instruction, then encourage the vendor to reduce the price.

The agent will usually tell you there and then, after looking round the property at some length, what they think a suitable selling price would be, but whether this is higher or lower than anticipated, it is you who finally decides the asking price. If you have researched the market well, you will be in the best position to decide on a price which is not too high or too low.

At the end of the day, like everything else, a property is only worth what someone is willing to pay for it. Some improvements can raise a property's value, but cost a relatively small amount of money. Conversely, it must be said that certain luxury improvements never recoup their cost. They may appeal to the present owners, but size and location are ultimately the most important factors in a selling price, so a two bedroom cottage will only ever achieve the higher end of the price bracket for such a building, regardless of expensive additions.

When agents visit to 'value' the property and offer their services, the vendor should have to hand a note of relevant details, including improvements and any legal restrictions relating to the property, as well as a list of any questions or queries regarding the sale in general and each agent's services.

TOP TIP

Do not be tempted to instruct an agent just because he claims to have a registered applicant desperately looking to buy a property exactly like yours. If you do, you should not be surprised if the desperate applicant suddenly changes his criteria the very day your property becomes available for viewing.

If you have carried out a lot of work and the agent has knowledge of the property before this work was carried out, he may base his valuation on the price you paid for it, plus the amount spent on improvements. Obviously this is neither fair nor accurate, and any agent suggesting it should be disregarded. Firstly, in a constantly changing market it is unlikely that a property's worth will remain static from one year to the next, and secondly the saleability of the property will have improved, making the theory unworkable.

TOP TIP

Notice how retailers avoid pricing in round figures. A shirt will be priced at £9.95 or a car at £9,950 because these figures appear considerably less than £10 or £10,000 respectively. Similarly, avoid pricing your property in round figures - £89,950 is only £50 off £90,000, but seems much less.

In readiness for an agency valuation, prepare the property with as much care as you will when presenting it to a potential buyer (see Chapters 2 and 3), paying particular attention to the front, a photograph of which usually accompanies the written details. The impression the agent gets of your property will be the one he or she gives to potential buyers who register with the agency. If you present the property well, the agent will be positive and enthusiastic when describing it, effectively recommending it above others.

After each agent has given their valuation and departed the scene, reflect on the way they appeared to you. Were they:

- On time?
- Neat and tidy?
- Polite?
- Enthusiastic? If they can't muster enthusiasm for you, they are unlikely to be able to do so for a buying customer.
- Professional and organised - did they have business cards, sample
  particulars etc.?
- On the ball - did they ask relevant questions and clarify their advertising strategy?
- In general agreement with your own opinion of value?

If you can answer 'yes' to the above, congratulations - you have found yourself a good agent.

The property details

Your chosen agent will take measurements of the property and prepare the written details. Read through these carefully, not only for mistakes but also for any relevant information which may have been overlooked. If you are lucky enough to have a unique selling point, make sure is it known. This could be anything from a granny annex to a view over the village green, but if some particular aspect of your property distinguishes it from all the others, it could be the very thing that sells it.

TOP TIP
Once instructed, get as many of the agency staff to come to the property as possible, so that all of them can accurately describe it to applicants.

It is usual for the agent to take a photograph of the property to accompany the details, but there is no reason why you should not supply your own if you think you can do a better job, as long as it conforms with certain requirements which the agent will clarify. When supplying your own photographs:

> **TOP TIP**
> Prepare an additional sheet of useful information about the property and the area, maybe in the form of an A to Z to be included with the agent's details. Include such things as nearest schools, churches, sports facilities, hospitals, transport links.

- Portrait angle should be avoided - stick to landscape (wide rather than tall).
- Take the photograph in good light; sunshine if possible.
- Don't have too many cars cluttering up the shot, but if you do include one (maybe to show the length of the drive), make sure it is clean.
- Take several shots from different positions.
- Open curtains or blinds.

Naturally the agents will need the negatives for reprinting purposes.Be warned – using photographs which are in any way deceptive causes a great deal of unnecessary frustration. If an applicant makes an appointment to view a property based on an impression given by a deceptive photograph, one of two things can happen when he arrives to see the property as it really is. Either he keeps the appointment out of good manners, wasting his time and yours since he has no intention of buying, or he takes one look at the reality of the situation and goes home.

On a final point concerning photographs, if the period of time your property is on the market spans the seasons from snowy Winter through to sunny Spring, you will need to arrange an updated photograph. This is because, whilst the snow makes an attractive picture, it reveals that the property has been on the market for some months and gives the impression that there 'could be something wrong with it' in the eyes of a prospective buyer.

DID YOU KNOW?   *0Council Tax Bands are often included on property details.*

Once the agent has compiled his written description of your property, he will give you a copy for your approval. Sadly, perusal of such wording, intended one would think to encourage enthusiasm in the reader, can be painfully disappointing and not the least bit inspiring. Admittedly, agents have experience of writing such material, but their grammar often lets them down and, more often than not, their effort to stimulate the reader into viewing fails miserably. The main reason for this is because an agent's experience comes from repetition, making for dull descriptions, each property sounding much like all the others.

So, whilst most of the agent's blurb might be satisfactory, the vendor should not be afraid to change or add to that which is not. Pay heed though, to the Property Misdescription Act which forbids the use of non-factual or misleading information. This basically means that 'delightful, sunny living room' should now read 'south-facing living room' (if, in fact, it is), omitting the writer's personal opinion and replacing it with fact. After all, 'a large garden' may seem large to someone used to a window box, but small to someone who is used to a house in 20 acres of grounds.

If you mention details of improvements, such as the installation of cavity wall insulation or a garage conversion, you will need to have current guarantees available for inspection and the agent (and later your solicitor) will need details of the planning consent and/or building regulation approval which relates to the work.

To ponder lightly the subject of misdescription for a moment, anyone who has looked over a clutch of property details prior to the Act, will have experienced imaginative narration at its best. Some of the descriptions are works of complete fiction and another book could be written on outrageous examples, but a personal favourite must be the statement which went along these lines:

"The cottage garden adjoins a peaceful area of the church
grounds which the previous owner has himself been involved in
cultivating with an abundance of flowers and spring bulbs."

Sounds lovely, but in reality the cottage backed directly onto a modern cemetery. The owner, it transpired, had sadly departed his garden, moving to the other side of the wall to cultivate spring bulbs – personally. Estate agents are not generally known for their tact or good taste, but if nothing else, the wit who wrote this had a sense of humour.

TOP TIP
Include a floor plan with your agency details, showing room measurements, door openings, windows etc. Some agents offer this service but they invariably make a charge for it, and most don't do a better job than you could do yourself.

Agency agreements

On instructing an agency to handle the sale of your property, you will probably be required to sign an Agency Agreement of some kind, which is a document setting out your obligations and those of the agent. These Agreements vary slightly from company to company, but generally cover the following:

1.Obligations of the Vendor:

• In the case of a sole agency agreement, the vendor cannot instruct any additional agents without first giving notice that he intends doing so, in which case the commission fee will often be increased. (See From Sole to Multiple Agency, Chapter 7).

• The vendor must give written notice if withdrawing the instruction.

• The vendor agrees to pay the agent's commission fee (commonly 1-3% + VAT). This fee becomes liable for payment on exchange of contracts, but in practice payment usually takes place on completion, deducted from proceeds of the sale.

2.Obligations of the Agency:

• The agency is required to ask if the vendor or his relatives have any connection with employees of the agency.
• The agency is required to advise of any financial services they offer to applicants, and will usually promise not to prefer one applicant over another solely because he or she has agreed to accept these services, for which the agent may receive a commission.

• To conform with the Property Misdescription Act, the agency should obtain the vendor's approval on the accuracy of the written details prior to their distribution. (This shifts responsibility for accuracy from the agency to the vendor, so do check the details carefully before approving them.)

DID YOU KNOW? *If you enter into a sole agency agreement but sell through another agent during the period of that agreement, you will be liable to pay commission to both the agent who introduced the buyer and the agent with whom you have the original agreement.*

Keeping up the pressure

Once you have approved the written details, call into the office to make sure they are well displayed. Also, it may seem sneaky, but you could ask a friend or relative to register with the agency as a potential buyer to ensure your details are being dispatched promptly and carry colour photographs, if that is what you have agreed.

You will have already discussed the amount of advertising offered, but check the proposed media coverage regularly to make sure you are happy with the advertisement itself and the frequency with which it appears. If not, complain.

> **TOP TIP**
> Promotion through the agency is your main, if not your only tool for reaching potential buyers, so it is imperative that you find an agent who is adept in promoting property.

Standard in staff employed as estate agents varies enormously. Some will be qualified surveyors with years of experience, some will be fresh out of school with no knowledge of selling property or anything else. The others will be somewhere in-between. You may be fortunate enough to find an agency which values training and encourages all their staff to learn new skills or, more commonly, your agency may only be in business because of the skill and effort of one or two individuals. Given this, you will probably discover one member of staff who stands out as the most competent, and you would do well to implore this person to handle all aspects of your sale. Explain that you have been particularly impressed by the way he handled this or that, and would feel more confident of finding a buyer quickly if he handled your sale personally. Estate agents are not ignorant of their poor image and rarely receive praise, so your comments will be welcome. Always address correspondence to your chosen individual, and if he is unavailable when you telephone, request that he returns your call rather than discuss the matter with the other staff. Most importantly, always speak to your chosen agent promptly after an applicant has viewed your property, so that you can be sure the applicant will be approached by a person who is capable of negotiating on your behalf.

When you first place your property with an agency, you will find the staff very keen to handle your sale. Sadly, their enthusiasm tends to diminish the longer a property remains on the market, so it is vital to keep yourself and your property fresh in the agent's mind. To do this, keep in close contact by calling into the office and/or telephoning regularly. Find out the names of all the staff and use them. Be pleasant and approachable, but do not become so friendly as to diminish your status as a valued client. Enquire regularly how your sale is progressing, and if the response to advertising is not producing a satisfactory number of applicants, ask what the agent's next step will be to encourage further promotion. If you appear unconcerned over progress with the sale, the agent will be too.

When to sell

Seasonal highs and lows are common in most types market places, and the property market is no exception. However, the priorities of homebuyers have changed over recent years to the extent that property is no longer seen as an investment and the fear of being unable to dispose of a property has made people far more cautious when searching for one. The current decline in the number of homebuyers has greatly reduced the type of 'impulse buying' which previously saw people rushing to buy at traditionally busy periods in the property calendar, and buyers are nowadays more concerned with getting the right deal at whatever time of the year it presents itself. Because properties are on the market for longer, the season in which they actually sell is not determined by the season they are first marketed, and a property which comes onto the market in the spring may not attract a buyer until the winter.

Traditionally, spring is the favoured time to place property on the market, with the hope of a sale before the start of the summer holiday season when shortages of staff in building societies, solicitors offices and estate agencies can cause delays. A sale in early autumn narrowly avoids the dreary winter months when even the best kept gardens can look unappealing, and, of course, Christmas. Specifically Christmas, in fact, since nowadays preparations for Yuletide celebrations start early in the year, many shops bedecked with tinsel as early as October, and the festivities don't die down until well into January.

The simple consideration when deciding what time of the year to sell a property (assuming you have a choice) is to choose the season which best suits the property's character and accentuates it's best aspects. Bear in mind 'though, that selecting the right agent will take time and, once selected, the agent will need time to prepare the property details for circulation (printing, developing photographs etc.) before the promotion can start. Vendors will therefore need to allow for a delay of around a month between the time they first approach agents for initial valuations and the time viewings commence.

TOP TIP

If you sell during busy holiday months, bear in mind that your solicitor could be away and that banks and building societies get short staffed, all of which can cause delays. Help yourself by finding out in advance who will deal with your paperwork in the case of absences and offer your assistance to save time, maybe by collecting important documents personally.

When to buy

DID YOU KNOW? *In 1991, the good people of the UK spent around £50,000m on housing, but over double that amount on alcohol and tobacco.*

If you intend to purchase a further property once your present one has been sold, you should ideally start looking for your next home as soon as possible, and not necessarily wait until you have found a buyer.

Many people feel unworthy to view other properties until their own is sold because they are not in a position to make an offer until they have a firm buyer themselves. Also, they fear that finding a suitable property will bring them great disappointment if the property is then sold to someone else before their own sale is secured. Estate agents often reinforce this timid approach, encouraging the idea that those who start to view early are at best naive and at worst time-wasters. It is not difficult to understand why agents adhere to this view when you consider that one of their major overheads is the distribution of property details. Whilst they are willing to bombard 'serious' applicants with dozens of details, they may not be so keen to send details to applicants who are not in an immediate position to buy.

So what is the point in starting to look for your next property before securing your own sale? After all, the owners of the properties viewed would be foolish to accept your offer until there is a firm commitment on your own sale, and it is very unlikely that the selling agents would recommend this. The agent will, quite rightly, advise his client to remain on the market until a buyer can be found who has received an acceptable offer or, better still, exchanged contracts.

But what happens when the tables are turned, and you are the client who receives a offer from a buyer who has already exchanged contracts? Not only will your buyer want to move quickly, but his favourable position will almost certainly encourage him to haggle down your price. If you have not found your next property where does this leave you? You may refuse to budge on your price (because at this point in time you do not know what funds you need to acquire your next home), which could well result in your buyer withdrawing his offer in favour of the next property on his list. Even if you can settle on the price, you will still need to explain that you have not found a suitable property, and hope that the buyer doesn't get jumpy and withdraw his offer through fear of loosing his own sale because of your delay. Your only option then, if you don't want to risk losing your buyer, is to visit all the local estate agents, gather up armfuls of written details, then hurriedly view as many properties as you can, running the risk of making a hasty and unsuitable purchase. All this hassle, simply because you were not prepared in advance.

A much happier scenario, on receipt of an acceptable offer, would see you calmly approach the vendor of the property you have selected as your next home and make a keen offer now that you are able to proceed, using your now favourable position to pass on any reduction in price on your own sale. If the first property on your list has already been sold, you will swallow your disappointment but be comforted that you have, of course, a second and third choice lined up in anticipation.

So don't be put off by estate agents who are full of initial enthusiasm to put you on their mailing list, but then become quite chilly when you admit that your house has not yet attracted a firm buyer. If you receive details of a property which seems to fit your requirements, go and take a look at it from the outside, which will tell you almost as much as viewing the inside. If the location is right and you feel it would be worth an internal viewing, arrange an appointment. If the vendor asks about your buying position, don't be abashed to say that you have not yet found a buyer; after all, neither has he. When you find the right property, speak with the vendor or his selling agents and say that you like the property very much, are unfortunately not able to make an offer at this time, but will get in touch again when you are in a position to do so. Most vendors will be pleased to hear that someone is interested in their property, even if they are disappointed that the sale is not imminent. The selling agent will be pleased to report that he is doing a good job for his client by finding interested applicants, and you will have lost nothing by the experience, but will be spurred on to do everything in your power to hurry along your own sale.

If you are moving within your local area, there is another very good reason why registering your interest as a buyer, at the same time as being a vendor, is useful. By presenting yourself to agents as a customer, you find out first hand their approach to applicants. The treatment you receive as a customer will be exactly the same treatment any potential buyer of your property receives so if, in your role as applicant, you discover your own agency is not dealing with your purchasing requirements in a satisfactory manner, you can change agents as soon as possible. Better to do so quickly than leave the property unsold for any longer than necessary.

TOP TIP

A measure of the selling agent's success is his 'applicant to sales ratio' so make sure yours is diligent with all applicants, and does not allow any possible buyers to slip through the net.

Selling and buying through the same agency

If the property you select as your next home is coincidentally being sold by your own selling agent, you are presented with several advantages. The first is that you have good reason to re-negotiate the commission you have agreed to pay on achievement of your sale, using the argument that you will indirectly be helping the agent achieve two commissions – your own and that payable by the vendor of the property you want to buy.

The prospect of a double commission, regardless of whether or not you have found a buyer yourself, also gives the agent an added incentive to bring your alliance with him to a speedy conclusion, which is obviously beneficial to you.

TOP TIP

Your selling agent will be keen to recommend any reasonable offer you make on a property they are also marketing.

- If you have found a buyer, the agent will be encouraged to recommend your (fair) offer to his other client. If his client rejects your offer the agent knows you may buy through another agent and he will then loose a sale.

- If you have not found a buyer, but show an interest in purchasing a property being marketed by your own selling agents, they may put extra effort into securing your sale so that you are in a position to proceed with the purchase.

Finally, assuming you have instructed agents worth their salt, they should be able to orchestrate much of the delicate timing involved in simultaneous selling and purchasing, and the number of agents involved in the process is reduced, thereby lessening the chance of confusion. In handling both your purchase and sale, the agent should be aware of any hiccups before they become major problems and, by having his finger on the pulse of proceedings, can make sure the whole transaction does not come to a grinding halt.

In summary:

- Appreciate your importance. You are the customer and have a right to demand, and receive, good service and results from your estate agent.

- Prepare the property with great care for a valuation. The impression the agent gets is the impression he will impart to applicants.

- Don't rely on the agents to set a reasonable value on your home. Listen to their opinions by all means, but make your own investigations before deciding on the current market value.

- Interview several, if not all, the agents in your area before deciding which one to give your custom to.

- Work with your agent, but don't imagine his efforts alone will sell your property.

- Read agency Agreements carefully. If you do not agree with something, discuss an amendment.

- Once an agency has been instructed, single out the most competent member of staff, and court his or her personal involvement.

- The written details which the agency compiles will be the first impression an applicant gets of your property. Scrutinise them before they are circulated, and amend as necessary.

- Prepare your own additional details with a floor plan, information on facilities in the area, transport links, etc.

- Keep a constant check on advertising. Make sure your property appears regularly in the local press and the printed details are displayed in the office.

- If possible, time the initial promotion of your property to fit in with the time of year when the property looks it's best.

- Start looking for your next property (if applicable) before finding a buyer for your existing one.

PREPARING FOR VIEWINGS

They say it's a buyer's market out there, which basically means that those in the fortunate position of having either sold their own property or being a first-time buyer with nothing to sell, are spoilt for choice. These lucky people will get dozens of agency details dropping through their letter box, most of which will be disregarded on the quality of the photograph alone. What this means to you, as a vendor, is that if you do not make every effort to attract these buyers, someone else will. Never forget that you are in direct competition with other similar properties on the market. So, before each viewing, you will need to allow sufficient time to prepare the property for inspection. Unless your home is permanently spotless and immaculately presented, you will need it.

This chapter covers some of the many points which help to make a property appealing to the buying public. None of the points taken individually will sell your home, but put them together and you increase the saleability by improving on the competition and showing the property in its best light.

First impressions

First impressions count, so the front of the property should aim to immediately attract. A 'For Sale' board will advertise the property as available, but it will be wasted advertising if the front of the property doesn't demand a second glance. Make sure the 'For Sale' board is not dirty or crooked (which gives the impression it has been there for a long time) and that it is clearly visible from whichever direction the property is approached. If there are any old 'Sold' boards on neighbouring properties, ask the relevant agents to remove them.

DID YOU KNOW? *The Department of Environment stipulates in rules regarding outdoor signs that 'Sold' boards must be removed not later than 14 days after completion of the sale.*

If you have a front garden make sure the lawn is kept mown and the weeds at bay. A hanging basket (summer and winter) or a few colourful tubs make a huge difference to a bare garden and cost very little. Also, they are not wasted because you can take them with you to your next address.

Complete external decoration is wonderful if you can afford it and think it will recoup it's cost, but simply giving a faded front door a new coat of paint will be a great improvement. You may even find that scrubbing down paintwork on windows and doors is enough. Whilst the soap and water is out, don't forget to wash any grubby net curtains; something which is often overlooked by vendors but never fails to give a lacklustre impression to potential buyers.

The back garden should be kept tidy with lawn mowed, patio swept, leaves cleared, weeds removed and hedges trimmed. If you have children, clear away their toys to avoid turning what should be a tranquil setting into something which looks like a public playground. If you have dogs, make absolutely sure there are no 'deposits' or old bones lying around. Garden furniture is inviting and should be cleaned (especially if it is white) and arranged attractively. If you have a nice view, position the furniture to show that the view is enjoyed and is a valuable part of the property.

The number one priority when aiming to attract potential buyers must be to make your property looks its best from outside. Pay attention to maintenance by all means; check drainpipes and clear the gutters, but at the end of the day there is simply no substitute for good looks. Some properties do sell in spite of their poor appearance, usually because they have a special feature like a spectacular view or occupy an unusual position, but although properties like these might sell eventually, you can safely assume they would have sold sooner, and probably fetched a higher price, if their appearance had been improved. No matter how strongly an agent recommends a property, no matter how often it is advertised, the visual impact it has on potential buyers is the greatest decider on whether or not it sells.

From the outside, a property has several opportunities to sell itself on appearance alone:

- A 'For Sale' board will be worthwhile advertising if passers-by like the look of a property and are prompted to request written details If they are not influenced by the appearance, they won't trouble to make further enquiries.

- The photograph on the written details will reaffirm the first impression of those who enquired through a 'For Sale' board Applicants receive large batches of estate agency details, so those which carry a good photograph of an attractive property stand out from the others and prompt an appointment to view.

- On arriving for a viewing, the impact of the written details is positively confirmed, and a good first impression is assured.

You can see from the above how a positive impression is achieved before an applicant even sets foot inside the property, which goes some way to explaining how one property on an estate sells quickly, whilst others for sale at the time, all basically identical in size and location, fail to find buyers. In situations like this, each seller is vying for attention with neighbouring properties, and the only way to win over the competition is either by lowering the price or making the property more visually appealing than the others. Often there is only one major difference between a house which sells and its neighbour which does not, maybe where plain windows have been replaced with something more attractive, but more often it is the overall outer appearance which makes a property stand out from all the others.

Creating the right welcome

The philosophy of this chapter centres on how to make your property look well cared for and appear inviting. Although price, location and size are the main requirements most buyers set out to meet, it is often the appearance and atmosphere of a particular property which actually sells it. So, once a prospective buyer makes an appointment to view your home, having presumably have found the price, area and size acceptable from the agency details, you are part way to securing a sale; it would be a shame to blow it with carelessness! Your aim should therefore be to make a favourable impression on as many of the buyer's senses as possible, but there is more to this than meets the eye, since he will not only be affected by what he sees, but also by what he 'feels'. When a person enters an unfamiliar environment (i.e. your home) he gets an overall impression from the general atmosphere of the place – whether it is warm, comfortable and welcoming, or cold, cheerless and hostile – and this elicits an emotional response. In other words, if you make a potential buyer feel 'at home' you positively influence his impulsive reaction to a pile of bricks and mortar.

DID YOU KNOW?   *Most people spend more effort preparing their home to impress dinner guests, than they do to tempt a buyer.*

When evaluating the immediate visual impact created inside a property, the first thing the vendor needs to do is imagine what a prospective buyer will see once he or she enters the property. Will a favourite picture in the hall be the first thing noticed, or is the eye more likely to be drawn to a patch of carpet worn through to the boards?

Most of us get so used to our surroundings that we no longer really see them. We would probably notice a picture hanging crooked or a lightbulb which had blown, and eventually these minor irritations would be corrected, but many other areas which could benefit from minor improvements often go ignored.

In a time when most people lead hectic lives, struggling to fit work, family and social activities into the limited number of hours in the day, our homes are often best arranged for convenience, rather than aesthetic appeal. Of course, in the normal course of life there is nothing wrong with this, but it will help the vendor if he sees the property as others will, so enabling identification (and correction, finances permitting) of as many negatives as possible to improve the general appearance.

It helps to go into each room armed with a notebook and jot down all the things you notice about the room in a list of positives and negatives. Be honest in your observations, but accept that you will not be able to change everything and need to prioritise. Look at each room in terms of decoration, flooring, furniture, soft furnishings, lighting etc.

Some of the changes you would like to make might not be possible, either because they are not cost effective or because you have neither the time or money to spare. Once you have made your lists, look through them carefully, then mark each in order of importance and cost, i.e. score the importance on a scale of 1 to 10, and the cost on a score of A to D. You can then easily identify those items marked 1A (important / low cost) which can be done immediately, and those items marked 8D (not vital and expensive to boot) which are probably best ignored, i.e.:

MASTER BEDROOM

	Present condition	Improvement	Score
Flooring	Presentable but plain	Use rug from lounge	1A
Lighting	Ceiling light - cold	Buy cheap bedside lights	3B
		Change bulb to lower watt	8A
Furniture	Fitted wardrobes	No change necessary	
	Bed	Move to show off	1A
	Seating	Re-upholster	8D
Wallpaper	Old and dull	Paint wallpaper - peach	1C
S.furnishings	Linen co-ordinated	No change necessary	
		Cushions for seating	4B

Do not imagine that all your observations will be negative. You will almost certainly re-discover plenty of positive points which have not been receiving their due attention until now. In the example list above, for example, the room houses a handsome antique bed which is not immediately noticeable when entering the room as presently arranged. Since this bed is a major focal point in the room and is worth showing off, it makes sense to rearrange the room to play up this positive feature. It costs nothing to make this type of alteration, just the imagination to notice that it is worth the effort.

TOP TIP

Don't be afraid to bring attention to any unusual aspects of your property. This gives the buyer a reason to remember yours over all the others he will see.

Furniture and effects

Does the arrangement of furniture in your home best suit the rooms? Today's modern homes are often short on space, so the arrangement of furniture is vital to ensure each piece fulfils its function without making the room look crowded and cramped. But it may be that the furniture is arranged for day to day convenience rather than to look it's best, in which case some moving around could be in order to ensure the best pieces of furniture are displayed to best effect. Perhaps the dining table, handsome as it is, is usually covered up because the children use it to do their homework on. However, if the dining table is worth showing, it would be more impressive during a viewing if it were polished and cleared of papers.

Expensive furniture is not the main requirement for showing rooms to their best advantage, nice though it is, but it *is* necessary to consider the arrangement of the furniture. This observation may baffle many readers. After all, a prospective buyer is viewing the property itself, not the furniture in it, so one would think that the arrangement of the furniture has little effect on the impression given during a viewing. Not true. The buyer will, of course, be looking at the size of the rooms and their state of repair and decoration as a priority. These are the things he or she will consciously make a point of observing. But the ambience of the room, its 'feel' and character, will not go unnoticed, and it could be precisely this which makes your home more attractive to a buyer than a similar one down the road.

Take for example a house which has a third reception room on the ground floor. The owner is a keen restorer of furniture and ordinarily uses this room as a storeroom. However, the room is quite large so, when selling the property, the owner recognises that leaving the room as a storeroom does not make the most of the accommodation as a whole. Accordingly, he moves the restoration work into the box room upstairs, and puts the bedroom furniture (previously crammed into the box room) into the third reception room. This bit of furniture swapping changes the original 'storeroom' into a good sized ground floor bedroom which gives a more appealing apportionment of space and, on the estate agent details at least, appears to increase the number of bedrooms.

Looking around your own home, you may well find that some of your furniture, conveniently placed for everyday life, could be more suitably positioned elsewhere, either to increase the feeling of space or simply to look more attractive. If you are determined to achieve the best price for your property in the shortest time, a little disruption in such a good cause is surely justified.

Often the smallest changes can make a difference to the general feel of a property. For example, you may always put your plants on the windowsill because they thrive there, but do they actually add to the room's appearance as they are, or do they hide a pretty window? Your living room furniture may be conveniently grouped round the TV, but would a different arrangement make the room appear bigger? And what about outside – is the garden furniture piled up in the garage when it could be more usefully employed as an attractive arrangement? There must be hundreds of such instances where furniture is not best displayed, so take the time to make sure yours is not ruining the feel of your home.

You will probably find that some furniture reorganisation, once tried, is preferable and may even make you wish you had thought of it long before. Some changes, however, may not suit your lifestyle, and while you can appreciate that the coffee table looks best in the middle of the room, it may not be practical there because your large dogs or small children are apt to bump into it. In instances like this you will need a plan of action so that, when an appointment is made for a viewing, you can effect the changes quickly and methodically instead of floundering around in a panic having forgotten what reorganisation you decided upon. Obviously you cannot move all your furniture around every time someone makes an appointment to view, but there may be one or two small changes which you can add to a Preparation List (see below) which are not unreasonable but make a big impact.

Sometimes home owners have lived in a property for so long they have forgotten its best points. If this sounds familiar, try to remember what made *you* buy it. It is very difficult to see your home, warts and all, as others will see it. So, if you can accept some personal criticism with good grace, enlist the help of friends (preferably those with excellent taste) and ask for their honest opinion and suggestions for alterations.

Windows and doors

Like moths to a light, people are invariably drawn to windows, so whether looking at or through, you can be sure viewers will make a beeline for them. Windows are often the focal point of a room, especially if there is no other core feature like a fireplace, so they deserve to be treated as such. Often taken for granted, but rarely ignored during a viewing by prospective buyers, windows are always worth paying particular attention to. Firstly, check that the frames and sills do not look tatty, giving a coat of paint if necessary, and always make sure the glass is clean.

TOP TIP

For summer viewings, leaving open french doors or windows which give view on to a pleasing garden appears to bring the outside inside and can increase the illusion of space.

As well as being a focal point to a room, windows should be utilised fully for their light giving quality. Attention should, of course, be given to artificial lighting, but natural light from windows must not be disregarded, and it is almost always advantageous to exaggerate this light wherever possible. A pale colourscheme bounces light back into a room, whereas dark colours seem to absorb it. Mirrors reflect light, especially when placed opposite or at right angles to a window, and if the mirror covers much of a wall (perhaps in a small hall or cloakroom) the amount of light in the room will be dramatically increased.

A suitably dressed window is an asset to any room. If the windows are unattractive, bulky or elaborate curtains can be used for concealment and the curtains then become a feature in themselves, but usually it is best to dress windows so as not to block out light. If net curtains are used for privacy or decoration, remember that they gather dust very quickly so washing them thoroughly (there are several products available which 'whiten' net curtains) will make them brighter. In some cases, for example if a window is a particularly attractive shape or has stained glass, it might be best to leave it unadorned.

> **TOP TIP**
> Take a look at pubs and hotels at night to see how inviting they look from the outside with lots of lighted windows. If you have a viewing in the evening, turn the lights on before your potential buyers arrive to achieve a similarly inviting glow.

On to doors, and the golden rule here is if they are not worth looking at, leave them open. However, if they are a selling point, like grand double doors which make a good entrance, show them off by using them.

DID YOU KNOW? *Half open doors make a room feel smaller. This is because, assuming the door opens inwards, a large object over 6ft tall has been brought into the room, taking up space. Close the door and you remove the object, it's as simple as that.*

No other decorated surface gets such a tough time as doors. If they are painted, a good wash down or a new coat of paint does wonders, and years of grimy fingerprints can easily be cleaned off handles and finger plates with a quick wipe.

Both doors and windows will benefit from being given a maintenance overhaul inside and out to make sure they are in good repair. Even assuming a potential buyer doesn't notice them, which is unlikely, a surveyor will. In extreme cases where the windows or doors are detrimental to the appearance of a property, replacing them might be an option which could add a great deal to the appeal of the property. However, replacement windows are extremely expensive, so the impact must be worth the cost to consider this option. (See Chapter 4, Improvements).

If you consider replacing an internal door, you may end up replacing them all, so that they match and the lone new door does not show the others in a bad light. Replacement external doors are available 'off the peg' through retail outlets, and can seem fairly cheap to buy. However, do not neglect to build the added expenses of painting/staining, door furniture and fitting etc. into the final cost before deciding if a replacement door is really as cheap as it first appears. Fitting a new external door invariably involves delicate adjustments to the new door itself and the existing frame, so unless you are adept at DIY and have the relevant tools, you will need to employ an expert to do the work, which could double the cost of the new door in carpentry fees.

Lighting

The type of artificial lighting used in a room does far more than simply illuminate. Depending on the type of lighting used, the mood of the room is dramatically changed, the 'temperature' is affected and the decoration and furniture become either highlighted or shaded to influence colour and texture. Good lighting plays tricks on the eye and can be used effectively to exaggerate space or diminish faults, either by 'washing' walls with light or creating areas of shade. Light and shade should ideally be balanced, giving each area or function of the room lighting which fits its requirements. In a living room which doubles as a dining room, for example, the dining table could be lighted subtly for decoration whereas the living area is given more functional lighting, or vice versa. A room which is evenly lit can be rather depressing and uninspiring, whereas pools of light bring atmosphere and individuality. There are lighting fitments to fit just about any requirements, and whilst putting in new sockets and replacing ceiling fitments would be expensive, bringing in an additional table lamp or changing a lampshade or the colour of light bulbs can create a different look immediately for little cost.

Temperature

A relatively small point, but worth mentioning just the same, is the overall temperature of the property. If the temperature is too cold, the atmosphere is unwelcoming, too hot and your viewer will be uncomfortable. The best solution is to keep rooms warm, but leave some ventilation to avoid a stuffy atmosphere.

DID YOU KNOW? *Colour greatly influences perception of a room's 'temperature'. At the top of the spectrum, dramatic reds warm and stimulate Yellow, with its ability to reflect light, is both warm and cheerful. A haze of green is restful and cool, whilst the tranquillity of blue is cool and relaxing.*

If you have open fires (and are not selling in the middle of a hot summer) they could be lighted for no other reason than decoration, since most people find a lighted fire emotionally pleasing. The same applies to any other decorative fires, which are not only attractive to look at but are an expensive feature worth promoting if included in the selling price.

Aroma

Perfumes, deodorants, air-fresheners, and hundreds of other aromas have been designed and manufactured to please one of our most basic senses, that of smell. What a shame then, with all those hundreds of products available, if your home emanates a less than pleasing aroma. Often we become so accustomed to a particular smell that we no longer notice it. We are aware of stale cigarette smoke or pet smells in someone else's home, but our own homely pongs go unnoticed, and unfortunately, like bad breath or body odour, other people don't mention it for fear of causing upset or hurt feelings. The only way to check if your home has an odour problem is to specifically raise the subject with a friend or neighbour and plead for their honest opinion.

Unfortunately the manufacturers of air fresheners have yet to come up with something that doesn't smell like, well, air freshener, with the possible exception of a good quality pot pourri. A strong air freshener is almost worse than the offending smell, making it obvious that something is being covered up. This 'cover-up' could naturally cause concern to a prospective buyer, who may speculate wildly over whether the drains are blocked or there is a major damp problem, when in fact the only smell being disguised is the dog's damp coat after a walk in the rain. A much better solution to air freshners is to polish something in each room an hour or so before a viewing, and wear a pleasant perfume (or after-shave) yourself. A squirt of toilet freshner in the bathroom is always a good idea, but bleach or disinfectant are best avoided.

DID YOU KNOW? *People who have an aversion to hospitals often give 'the smell' as the reason for their discomfort when entering one. This shows the extent to which an unpleasant smell can offend our sensitivities.*

Returning to pet smells, remove all feeding bowls and put bedding away in a cupboard during proceedings. If you are unsure whether your animals are making your home smell, the next time they are left at home for an hour or so, restrict them to one room with the door closed. When you return, the smell (if there is one) will have been confined and become immediately apparent on entering the room. Amongst a dog's repertoire of delightful and charming habits is public flatulence, causing deterioration of air quality in seconds. If your dog chooses flatulence as a way to impress visitors (don't they all?) it would be advisable to leave him or her in a secure garden during viewings if possible.

Turning to smells which have a positive effect, the aroma of fresh filter coffee has been well publicised as a way to create an inviting atmosphere, so most people know about it. However, even if applicants who view your property are aware of this ploy, their subconscious is still impressed so there is no reason not to fill your home with such a pleasant aroma. If you want an alternative to coffee, one of the nicest smells is fresh baking. Choose a simple recipe which is neither complicated nor produces much washing-up, and have your baking conveniently, but unobtrusively, cooling by the time the viewer arrives. Not only does home made baking produce a wonderfully warm smell, but it tastes great too. Be careful if you decide to opt for anything other than coffee or baking – no matter how much you like the smell of garlic or frying bacon, these smells do not work in the same way.

TOP TIP

Some freshly ground dry coffee sprinkled onto a saucer and placed on top of a cupboard gives the same pleasing aroma as brewed coffee, but is less obvious.

Noise

If you have children living in your immediate vicinity, try to arrange viewings during the school day when they will not be making a nuisance of themselves in adjacent gardens or, worse still, in the road outside your home. It would be quite wrong to deceive a prospective buyer into thinking that no children live near, and most people accept a certain amount of noise from neighbouring children and adults alike. However, during a viewing you can rely on little Johnny next door to have a noisy tantrum, even if you never usually hear a peep out of him. It you have a good relationship with your neighbours, you could let them know of each viewing and ask them, very nicely, to limit any unnecessary noise for an hour or so during that time.

Town and city vendors who are subjected to noise pollution from the rumble of traffic on busy roads, will naturally close their windows during a viewing. This is not to mislead prospective buyers, after all they will notice any traffic noise on arrival at the property, but if good windows have been fitted in defence of outside noise and are shown as effective in use, the lack of noise inside the property could give it a positive advantage over others in the area which do not have such effective sound insulation.

DID YOU KNOW? *In one memorable Court case, a noisy neighbour drove a man to kill. The perpetrator of the noise was actually a parrot, who's persistent hue and cry infuriated his neighbour into entering the aviary and seeking his revenge by strangling the bird. In defence of the dastardly deed Council officers recorded the parrot noise levels to be equivalent to thunder.*

When it comes to orchestrating noise inside the home, recall for a moment those shops where the sales staff are clearly more interested in chattering amongst themselves or listening to the radio than they are in serving customers. If they manage to sell anything at all in these shops, it is in spite of these unhelpful staff, not because of them. The reason for mentioning this is to give some idea of the poor impression given to a prospective buyer during a viewing if a loud television or radio dominates proceedings. There is nothing wrong with family life continuing as normal, and certainly viewers do not want an audience whilst they look around, but the inaffable situation where the prospective buyer is completely ignored, or treated as an inconvenient intruder, is to be avoided. Televisions and radios, designed as they are to hold the attention, are difficult to ignore, so by allowing your attention to be diverted you will not be concentrating fully on the job in hand, i.e. showing your property in all it's glory and using your selling skills. If you must have the television on, maybe to keep small children entertained, turn the volume down so that the sound does not dominate any conversation you might have with a prospective buyer. If the buyer is himself distracted, he will not be concentrating on the viewing either, so your property will not remain prominent in his memory for long.

TOP TIP

Think of the person viewing your home as a valued customer and give him or her your undivided attention, taking full advantage of the opportunity to discuss the product on offer – your property.

Preparation list

Having taken an objective look at the property and identified what you need to do in preparation for a viewing, you might find that some of your preparations need to be done at the last minute so it will be helpful to compile a list to ensure that nothing is overlooked. Make a mental note of how long it takes to complete all the tasks on the list, so that you know how much time is needed to get the property ready for inspection. If the selling agent telephones to make an appointment for later that same morning, and you know it is not possible to prepare the property in time, ask for a later appointment. Few serious buyers insist on a 'now or never' appointment, but if there is a genuine reason for a viewing appointment at short notice, i.e. the buyer is in the area only briefly, it would be wise to accept the appointment, do as much preparation as you can, then hope for the best.

The outside of the property should, of course, be permanently in order. Prospective buyers will see the outside unbeknown to you, and if it does not live up to the photograph on circulated agency details, they may not bother to make an appointment to view inside. However, there may be one or two things you need to remember before each viewing, like turning on the outside lights or making a parking space available, so you could add these to the list as well.

Below is a list made for a recent sale, but you will obviously need to modify this for your own needs.

THINGS TO DO:
- Put cream arm covers on chairs and swap cushions for best ones
- Light fire (winter)
- Brew coffee
- Put dog bowls away and dogs in car
- Make up bed with best cover
- Set dining table (evening or Sunday lunch)
- Put washing line in garage
- Wipe garden table and chairs
- Turn lights on in kitchen, dining room and hall

In summary:

- Stay ahead of the competition by preparing the property as well as it possibly can be for viewings.
- Be aware of the importance of first impressions and remember that, once made, a bad impression it will be very difficult to erase or change.
- Cleanliness and tidiness cost virtually nothing to achieve and set the tone for a property which is well maintained and enjoyed by the present owners - exactly the impression you want to impart to potential buyers.
- Assess each room with a critical eye. Be objective in your observations, aiming to see what a potential buyer will see.
- Draw up a preparation list so that you will not overlook anything when getting ready for a viewing.

MAKING THE MOST
OF EACH ROOM

It seems the vast majority of prospective buyers decide if a property is not for them within the first few minutes of entering it. That is not to say that people don't become more (or less) interested as they move from room to room if they initially have no strong feelings either way, but an instinctive negative is pretty well immediate. Always remember that a poor impression at the beginning of a viewing is extremely difficult to erase. Create the right feel from the start, and your prospective buyer will simply become more and more convinced as he goes on to view the rest of the property, that this is the right place for him.

The object of this chapter is to encourage vendors to look at each room in their home afresh, to see if the saleability of the property and the price it will command can be improved upon by small alterations. Buyers will be looking to get the most they can for their money, so the size of rooms will probably be important to them. However, size and space are entirely different things: size is literal, the measurements, whereas space is more of a feeling. Two identically sized rooms can therefore give quite differing feelings of space, and hopefully this chapter will be helpful to vendors who want to increase the space in their rooms. For those selling a property with large rooms, the chapter will hopefully give a few hints on how to utilise the space to its full advantage.

You may decide that a particular room is the main selling point of your property, and hence deserves a complete overhaul. However, the general assumption in this chapter is that readers will want to avoid major improvements, so all the information given here is geared towards low cost additions or alterations. Wherever possible, purchases have been limited to those which can be taken to your next home.

41

There are dozens of books and magazines available on the subject of interior design, packed with ideas to inspire, so if you have never read one before, now might be the time to do so, but try not to get carried away with what you read. When selling a property there is no point in undertaking expansive and expensive decorating or improvement projects which will not add to the selling price. All you want to do is eradicate anything which decreases the value or reduces the chances of finding a buyer, whilst making the most of what you already have. Firstly, look at the rooms objectively to see if there really is a problem, and remember that a distinct improvement to one room, could be detrimental to another. For example, repainting a dreary room will undoubtedly be an improvement, but the same paint treatment used to cover expensive wall paper just because you are tired of it, will be a waste of time and money. You must decide what the rooms are lacking, if anything, and tackle any problems with as little upheaval and cost as possible. If the room is dull, creating light will be a priority, if the room is small you will be looking to increase the feeling of space, and if a room is bare you might like to look at ways of making it more comfortable. Be reassured, whatever the problem, there is a solution or at least an improvement. All it takes is dedication, enthusiasm and a bit of imagination.

Welcoming halls

The hall, as the second part of the property a prospective buyer sees (the exterior being the first), is one of the most important areas to work on when aimingh to convey a good impression. If you have a large hall, consider making greater use of it by including a desk or seating area, but avoid too much clutter as this will detract from the positive aspect of space

If the hall is small, a large mirror could well be the answer to increase the space by illusion, but position it carefully – the last place for a mirror in a long, narrow hall is at the end, which will just make it appear even longer and narrower. The best position for a mirror is opposite, or at right angles to, a source or light, effectively doubling it. Mirrors do not need to be expensively framed, especially when using strips of mirror glass which work well and can be more interesting than one large sheet. A glass merchant will supply mirror glass cut to size and often delivers as well, which is a valuable service to avoid breakage or hazards in transportation.

Lighting in a hall is important, and should aim to be warm and welcoming. A dull, gloomy hall does little to inspire hopes that the rest of the property will be any better, so it pays to make the area well illuminated, even in daylight. A desk lamp will create an intimate atmosphere, and brings attention to a seating or desk area. However, a single table lamp probably will not illuminate a hall sufficiently, so background lighting may be required as well.

Coat stands and hooks, whilst useful as a dumping ground for umbrellas, bags and all manner of outer wear, take up valuable space if overloaded, so now is a good time to put away those items which are rarely used. Don't neglect the cupboard under the stairs if you have one. Make sure it is tidy, and remember that it could be a selling point for conversion to a WC or compact office.

Kitchens to cook in

Generally speaking, in any room the less clutter the better, and this is certainly true of the kitchen. Forget for the moment that good cooks need everything to hand – for the purposes of selling your home, the rules are changed. You only need to visit a show-home to realise just how disordered the average kitchen is in comparison, but it is not the reduced amount of clutter on display in these professionally arranged rooms that is important; but which items are displayed. For some reason, many of us ignore the opportunity to make our kitchens attractive, reserving our most pleasing possessions for display in reception rooms, leaving the kitchen purely functional. We make every effort to clear away those items which are less than attractive in other rooms, but then allow the kitchen to become a mess of old cereal packets, washing up bottles and wet tea towels. But it needn't be like that. Why not put up a small shelf for cookery books, instead of leaving them in an untidy pile or jammed into drawers? Why not put up a few pictures and include a pretty rug? Many plants thrive in the atmosphere of kitchens, so these could also be included, and a display of indoor herbs in terracotta pots is both attractive and fitting, as are bowls of fruit, nuts or colourful vegetables. Open up the cupboards in your kitchen, see what is attractive enough to display and bring it out, then put everything else away behind closed doors.

DID YOU KNOW? *In over 80% of British households, men take responsibility for repairing household equipment. Since vacuum cleaners have been breaking down since 1907 and electric stoves since 1896, they should be quite good at it by now.*

Having taken a long hard look at your kitchen and noted the impression it gives, you may decide that it needs a face lift. Replacing the units is a very expensive option so you need to be sure this would be cost effective (see Chapter 4). A cheaper alternative might be to replace only the cupboard doors, and various styles are available nowadays from DIY stores and specialist shops. Unless your kitchen units are very old or were custom made to peculiar dimensions, you will probably be able to find replacement doors that fit. If you replace some doors but leave others, you could paint all of them to match.

If your kitchen is big enough to squeeze in some form of seating, why not do so, even if it is only a tiny table and a couple of chairs. Round tables can take up more room, but fit into corners snugly and are easy to walk around. By including seating, your printed property details will describe the room as a "kitchen/breakfast room" or "kitchen with dining area", instead of simply 'kitchen', thereby making more of the room.

TOP TIP

An old table, covered in some inexpensive fabric, matched with some of the same fabric made into curtains makes a kitchen instantly more comfortable and not just a place to cook.

If you do not have room for a table and chairs, the arrangement of your kitchen units may, with a little imagination, lend themselves to creating a breakfast bar. The simplest way to do this is to extend an appropriate part of the worktop and use high stools for seating. During a viewing, set the breakfast bar for a simple meal so that it is attractive and it's purpose does not get overlooked.

Living rooms to lounge in

The living room is, for many people, the most important room in the house, and definitely one to spend time looking at objectively to see if any improvements can be made. It is usually the room used most widely and, unlike most other rooms which have a single primary use, the living room often has to fulfil many functions. It is a place for relaxation, yet it may also be a place for work or study, as well as for entertaining guests. It is a room with scope for creating mood and giving your home character, and could be the room which makes the biggest impact on your viewers. Or not, as the case may be.

The importance of the living room, and the range of roles it must fill, usually dictates that it is the largest reception room. It also dictates that the standard of decoration should be good. Whilst a buyer might be prepared to forgo using the spare bedroom or study until he has time to decorate them, he will expect the living room to be habitable immediately.

If, having looked at the living room in your home, you decide that the decor has seen better days, you might do well to consider redecoration. This needn't be expensive or elaborate; a new coat or paint or touching up the existing decoration could be all that is needed to achieve an immediate improvement.

Many wallpapers can be painted, so there is no need to embark upon time-consuming and messy paper stripping. The safest colours, those which will appeal to most people and offend the least, are pastels, cream and good old magnolia, which will also serve to make the room appear light and airy. If you want to use a darker colour, try to co-ordinate it within a colour already evident in the room, maybe in the curtains or carpet. Above all, don't be afraid of paint. Old wooden chairs, picture frames and even light fittings can be successfully painted and given a new lease of life, and if you change your mind about the colour, you can always go over it with another.

When the time for spring cleaning comes around it is always a source of amazement to see how much dust and grime has accumulated, and what a difference cleaning it off makes. It costs virtually nothing to wipe down wallpaper (test a small patch first to check colour fastness), but you will find the shade and texture come alive again. Ceilings in homes where people smoke become stained very quickly, so cleaning them will also make a difference, but be prepared for neck ache! A corner of peeling wallpaper or chipped paint on the skirting creates such a dull impression, but can easily be rectified by paying a little attention to detail. If spare rolls of wallpaper and cans of paint were kept after the decorating was originally done, you should have plenty available for touching up minor areas of damage, so there will be no financial outlay.

> **TOP TIP**
> When repairing a patch of damaged wallpaper, always tear the replacement paper to size – never cut it as a blunt edge does not blend in with the remaining paper. Hold the paper in both hands with the pattern facing out, then tear towards you with one hand, creating a tapered edge. If the original paper hasn't faded too much, the repair will be virtually invisible.

One of the easiest ways to totally change a room's appearance, especially the living room, is with soft furnishings. If the room is dark and needs a lift, introducing a lighter colour scheme by changing the curtains and using a swathe of fabric over a chair or settee will do much to bring light and added comfort. Sofas and chairs can be obtrusive pieces or furniture which dominate a room and take up valuable space, but you can make them less conspicuous (especially if they are not worthy of the attention they command), by using loose covers of a similar colour to the carpet or walls so that they blend in with their surroundings. Matching cushions and curtains give a pleasingly co-ordinated effect, and if you are handy with a needle a few cushion covers will take very little time to make. Buying new curtains, especially if they are large, is costly so you may not want to include them in the selling price. When replacing curtains, bear in mind the following:

- Buy or make the curtains extra large to make sure they fit somewhere in your new home. Small, custom made curtains are unlikely to fit anywhere other than the window for which they were intended.

- If the curtains do not need to be drawn closed, but are more of a dressing, you may be able to get away with looping the material around a rail, instead of actually cutting and sewing. This is easier, requires less fabric, and leaves it un-cut to be used in your next home.

- In some stores, buying curtains ready–made is cheaper than buying the same fabric and making them yourself. This is one of life's little mysteries, but knowing it could save a lot of time and trouble.

Mirrors play a large part in increasing space, especially if they are floor to ceiling size. Placed in an alcove or on either side of a chimney breast, they give the impression that another room lies beyond, and of course they reflect light.

Finally, experiment with the arrangement of your furniture, since it is the arrangement as much as the furniture itself which gives the room its personality:

- Chairs lined up alongside each other look rather unsociable, whereas a grouped arrangement speaks of social interaction.

- Side tables with reading lamps suggest that this restful activity goes on in the room.

- Several individual sources of light clarify furniture arrangements which aim to separate a room into distinct areas of, say, seating/eating/study.

- If the room is long and narrow, placing a rectangular piece of furniture like a settee or table lengthways will only serve to increase the proportions, whereas by turning it widthways the room seems to gain width.

- If you consider adding to or replacing your seating, don't overlook wicker or cane furniture which is fairly cheap and, because it is not solid, does not take up too much space, nor do tables with glass tops.

> **TOP TIP**
> Clearing the floor can increase the feeling of space, so instead of positioning large items of furniture in the middle of the room, try putting them against a wall. If you have rugs, removing them shows a clear expanse of floor which can also make the area seem larger.

Dining in style

In these days of fast food and frantic living, we often find ourselves eating on the run or dining off a tray in front of the TV. However, most of us sit down to eat sometimes, and the great thing about creating eating areas in the home is that they can be virtually anywhere. A small table and chairs in a bedroom hints of intimate breakfasts; a large family table tells of lively gatherings; and looking at a formal dining arrangement you can almost hear the clink of crystal. Creating a dining area, maybe by squeezing a table into a hall or conservatory, makes the most of available space, and if the table is isolated from it's surroundings with localised lighting, the area becomes separated into a 'room' where previously there was none.

> **TOP TIP**
> If your dining area is unconventional, setting the table makes it's role obvious.

If you are fortunate enough to have a separate dining room for entertaining, then an evening viewing is an opportunity to make this room particularly attractive. You may not be expecting dinner guests, but can give the impression that you are by getting out the best china and making sure the table is dressed to kill. You can, of course, do this for a viewing at any time of the day, but you might do well to think up some plausible reason why your table is set for dinner at ten o'clock in the morning, or risk giving the game away as an obvious ploy to impress.

Most of us do not have the luxury of a separate dining room, but use instead a living/dining room or kitchen/dining room arrangement. In a living/dining room, especially if the area set aside for dining is small, you might prefer to show that the dining area is not a dining area all the time, but has dual usage; perhaps as a work table or for decorative display of plants and photographs. If the dining table takes up too much room, you might consider reducing its normal size by dropping the leaves (if the type of table allows this), and removing some of the chairs. You could then use the chairs to create a separate seating/eating area somewhere else in the house, perhaps with a small table in the bedroom.

Prospective buyers viewing a home which has a dining area in the kitchen will not relish the idea of eating or entertaining in the dining area if it is overshadowed by a kitchen which is anything less than spotless. Creating a division between the two functions of a kitchen/dining room gives each area impact and distinguishes it by character as well as function. A cabinet, dresser or rectangular table could be used as a division between a kitchen and dining area, and if the flooring is the same in both areas a rug under the dining table also suggests a division, as does lighting which illuminates each area independently.

> **TOP TIP**
> Sometimes a wall between two rooms is removed to create one
> dual purpose room, leaving part of the original wall as a divider.
> If the dividing wall is obtrusive, you can make it 'disappear' by
> using mirror (strips or tiles) on the facing sides.

Where a property has a living room or kitchen which is suitable (i.e. big enough) to take the dining furniture and so free up the room usually used for dining, this gives flexibility to the accommodation, effectively providing an extra reception room which prospective buyers may or may not imagine using as a dining room. Also, in a bungalow or flat where the accommodation is all on one level, advantage can be taken of the versatility this allows when compiling the estate agent's written details. Many vendors of single storey homes move the dining furniture into the living room or kitchen, and then show the dining room as an extra bedroom, particularly if the property has only one or two bedrooms. Some vendors don't move the furniture, but simply suggest to applicants at the time of viewing that the dining room could alternatively be used as a bedroom, which is why it has been described on the details as 'dining room/bedroom 2". Since the value of a property is roughly calculated on the number of bedrooms, this could increase the selling price.

Bathrooms

The most positive way to view the prospect of updating a tired looking bathroom is to console yourself that any alteration will usually be on a small scale, making it comparatively quick and cheap. Replacing the existing floor covering in a small bathroom, for example, will not break the bank, or you could even paint or sand down floorboards (if they are in good condition) and soften the look with a warm rug. Carpet is luxurious, and the type specifically made for bathrooms, because it does not need to be particularly hardwearing, can be purchased very cheaply. If you decide to buy new floor covering, look out for off-cuts or roll ends in carpet shops, and price up the various tiles available: cork, carpet, vinyl etc..

Today's bathrooms are more than the cold, severe rooms they used to be, helped in part by the huge array of different decorating products available. Wall tiles alone come in countless styles, colours and sizes, and for every one of these there are a dozen imaginative ways it can be used. Removing old tiling is an ambitious project, not least of which because you might find that the previous owners of your home used the tiles to cover unsightly or damaged plaster. A cheaper and quicker solution is to paint them. This is easier and more effective than it sounds, and either egg-shell or gloss paints work well (a good decorating shop will point out suitable products). It is vital that the tiles are thoroughly cleaned to remove any grease which may have accumulated on the surface, but after painting and applying a coat of polyurethane the effect is stunning and has the added advantage of covering old grouting at the same time.

TOP TIP

Transfer bathsalts and shampoos from cheap plastic containers into pretty glass ones. You can even use old jam or coffee jars, prettied up with circles of fabric secured over the top of the jars with ribbon. A collection like this makes an attractive display out of previous disarray.

If your bathroom suite desperately needs replacing, you might be able to find one advertised for sale in your local paper (be prepared to make your own arrangements to collect it though), or alternatively you may justify the cost of replacing one or two items or even the whole suite. Builders merchants and DIY shops are often the cheapest suppliers, but price the suites carefully because the range of costs is enormous, and bear in mind that individual items can prove more expensive than a complete suite. Modern suites come in a variety of colours and styles, with something to suit everyone; the plainest ones will usually be the cheapest, although strangely enough, white suites often carry an extra cost.

TOP TIP

With the popularity of 'period' furnishings, a range of decorative taps is available which give character to plain bathroom suites.

The family bathroom is possibly the most disordered room in any house. The floor is littered with discarded towels, the linen basket overflows with dirty washing and old toothpaste tubes jostle for space with various bottles and jars of lotions and potions. But there is no reason why the bathroom should not be a comfortable room. If you have space, a chair and small table will add interest as well as providing a suitable surface for displaying attractive bottles or a lush plant. Pictures and shelves give aesthetic relief to clinically tiled walls, and a few metres of low cost fabric could admirably cheer up (and cover up) the window. Alternatively, plain coloured window blinds, of the type you trim to fit yourself, are inexpensive and can be stencilled to co-ordinate with an existing colour scheme.

Shower curtains can be a decorative addition to the bathroom, or they can be an eyesore, depending on their state. If you have a shower curtain which has seen better days, it might be worth investing in a new one, and during a viewing you should make sure it

53

is neatly arranged and is not dripping water on the floor. If you don't use a shower curtain, but need something to soften an austere room, a swathe of fabric or lace draped like curtains from a pole over the bath will add interest and warmth.

It should go without saying that the bathroom and WC must be spotless and sweet-smelling. Avoid anything too personal lying around, like wet flannels and medical preparations. Watch out for condensation on the windows or tiling (chammy leather is particularly good for wiping moisture away without leaving smears), and don't forget to show the (tidy) airing cupboard.

And so to bed

On average, we spend one third of our lives in bed, asleep, but when considering the many other demands on a bedroom; for relaxation, dressing, reading, etc., we must appreciate that potential buyers look at bedrooms not only in terms of their suitability for sleeping, but also for fulfilling other functions. So, whatever the size of your bedroom, be sure to take advantage of available space to make the room more than just a place to sleep. You might be able to fit in a small table and chairs for cosy breakfasts or as a dressing table, and including a table lamp will make the lighting softer than an overhead light alone. If you don't have room for a table, you could improvise with a shelf at thigh level. Put a nice big mirror on the wall above the shelf, include a small chair, and you have a dressing table which can be fitted neatly into a tiny corner and takes up very little space.

In most homes, especially modern ones, bedrooms are small, with scarcely enough room for the essentials, so you will be treading a delicate path between fully utilising space and overcrowding. However, if you are lucky enough to have excess space, you might like to make greater use of it by partitioning off a section of the room with, for example, open bookcases used as display cases which work well because they do not obstruct light, whereas a solid piece of furniture or partition wall will. The newly defined area could be utilised in a host of ways; as a dressing room, study, seating area or even a nursery.

Whether the bedrooms in your property are large or small, light or dark, elaborate or sparse, comfort is what most buyers will be looking for, so the aesthetics of these rooms should be prominent in your mind when you review them, remembering that there is more to comfort than elaborate soft furnishings and deep pile carpets. The 'feel' you create in a bedroom is not derived from decoration alone, it comes from little touches that give the room a personality. A bedroom is, after all, personal. It is a haven away from the rest of the family, where peace and privacy are paramount, and it is this image you should aim to portray when inviting a potential buyer to view your bedrooms, and there are dozens of ways you can do this.

TOP TIP

Generally speaking, the size of bed dictates whether a bedroom is considered a double or single.

Start with the bed: it is usually the biggest single item in the room and therefore draws the eye. If your bed linen has seen better days, investing in a new quilt cover or bedspread will make a big difference. You might like to consider keeping your most attractive bed covers especially for viewings, then you know they will be washed and ironed (and not lying in a crumpled heap at the bottom of the laundry basket), ready to be switched with those in continual use when an appointment to view is made. If you can't run to the expense of new bed linen, a cheaper alternative would be to dye the covers you already have, and you could also consider dying the curtains to match. If you do not feel confident of using dying products at home, speak to your local dry cleaner who will give you advice, or ask them to do it for you. Sheets are one of the most inexpensive ways of buying large amounts of material, and these can be cut up and made into pillowcases or cushions, maybe a tablecloth for a small table, or used to cover tired bedside cabinets. One or two plain sheets, utilised in this way, will give a whole range of co-ordinated soft furnishings at very low cost.

TOP TIP

Good hotels know that little touches like fresh flowers, fluffy towels and bowels of fruit impress their guests and make them feel welcome, so take a tip from them when you prepare your bedrooms for viewings.

Pay attention to detail in bedrooms, arranging functional items with as much care as decorative ones. An untidy assortment of cosmetics for example, will not look attractive, whereas an arrangement of perfumes in pretty glass jars will. Piling toiletries etc. into one large container, maybe a wicker basket or fruit bowl, keeps them to hand whilst avoiding clutter.

Mirrors are a necessity in bedrooms, so you will probably already have some for making up and dressing, but take a close look at them to make sure they are making full use of their ability to reflect light and increase the feeling of space. Wardrobes with mirror doors are excellent; they make the wardrobes themselves disappear and when covering a length of wall, appear to double the room size. Framed mirrors, whilst both functional and highly decorative, are expensive.

However, you can make your own at a fraction of the cost by attaching mirror glass to the wall and creating your own frame:

- Decorative adhesive borders need not be limited to use under coving, although if you use them in this way, as well as to frame a mirror, the effect is especially pleasing.

- Depending on your artistic ability, paint can be used directly on the wall around a mirror. The simplest method is to carefully outline the mirror using one or two shades of paint which contrast with the colourscheme of the room. Stencils give the suggestion of a frame or, for the more ambitious, you could paint a 'picture' of a frame, complete with shadow and wood grain.

- Most DIY stores sell strips of beading which, when cut to shape and attached to the wall around the glass, are almost indistinguishable from the usual method of framing.

Children's rooms are a challenge just to keep clean, let alone tidy, but if you want to show them to their best advantage it is necessary to make sure they pass inspection at each viewing. Bear in mind that your potential buyer may not have children, in which case he will not be looking at these rooms with a view to continuing their existing use. If the rooms are covered in posters and only fit for teenage occupation, a potential buyer will have to allow for the cost of redecoration in his financial calculations.

TOP TIP
Unsightly radiators blend into walls when painted in
the same colour.

The spare or guest bedroom should not be overlooked, but you can console yourself that at least it will only need to be prepared once – if not in regular use, once made ready, it will remain so. Don't neglect this room just because you rarely use it yourself. Your buyer will have great plans for it, maybe even as the master bedroom, so it should be presented with care. Make the bed up, lay out fresh towels, include a plant or some flowers, in fact anything you would supply for the comfort of a guest.

TOP TIP
When preparing the spare bedroom, imagine a visitor
will be using it.

In an effort to endorse the feeling of comfort, the bedrooms should be warm, but be aware of musty smells which can linger and will spoil all efforts made to create a pleasing atmosphere.

Storage is very important in bedrooms, so if you are including any storage cupboards in the purchase price, mention them as a selling point. Most new houses come complete with built in cupboards, so if your buyers are moving from a new house, they are unlikely to have any wardrobes of their own and will be relieved of the expense of buying cupboards if you are leaving yours.

Home buyers demand more and more from properties nowadays, and en-suite bathrooms, previously a luxury reserved for good hotels, have now become commonplace. If you have en-suite facilities, you will naturally show them off, having first prepared the room with as much care as the main bathroom. If you do not have ensuite facilities, but do have enough room for them (take a look round a showhome to see how little space is needed to squeeze in a shower and WC), you could bring the possibility of installation to the attention of a prospective buyer during viewing. Ensuite facilities could be something the buyer is keen to have, but your property will still be in the running if the absence is rectifiable. If nothing else, it shows that your property is versatile. Replacing an existing bathroom suite can be well worth the outlay, but the high cost of installing plumbing where there was none before will probably not make the addition of ensuite facilities a cost effective improvement worth undertaking.

In summary:
- Don't underestimate the effectiveness of paint for a quick and easy face-lift.
- Get inspiration and practical advice from magazines and books on design and decoration.
- Isolate problem areas and decide on the importance of each. Time and money will be factors to consider, so use an Effort-to-Impact equation to see where time and money would be most effectively spent.
- Make the best use of available space.
- Be aware of lighting, which should be adequate and welcoming.
- Decide which room is most suited to which function, and rearrange furniture if necessary.
- Pay attention to detail when arranging plants, ornaments, pictures.

IMPROVEMENTS

Are they cost effective?

Most of the suggestions in the last chapter are relatively inexpensive and quick to put into effect. However, the vendor may decide that some areas of the property demand more substantial improvement, either in order to achieve a better selling price or else to make the property appeal to a wider audience. Before taking on any major improvements or alterations, it is important to make sure that money is not wasted on costs which will not achieve these goals. This will depend on:

- The type of property – does it have the potential to significantly increase its value?

- The current state of the property – are improvements or alterations really necessary? The cost of external repainting will be of little added benefit if the paintwork was in a fair condition to start with.

- The estimated value after improvements – is the value likely to be significantly increased? Where there are similar neighbouring properties on the market (on an estate perhaps), the one with certain improvements may sell quicker, but a rise in the final selling price is limited by the value of the neighbouring properties.

- The cost of the improvements and their effect.
  Some improvements are more expensive than others, yet have a limited impact on the value.

To decide if improvements are worthy of their cost, it is necessary to work out the 'value to cost' ratio, which basically means you need to ascertain whether the value is increased significantly enough to justify the cost.

EXAMPLE - VALUE TO COST RATIO:

			£
Present value		£	60,000
Improvements:	Kitchen	2,000	
	Painting outside	1,200	
	Internal decorating	800	
	New front door	250	
		4,250	
Estimated value after improvements			72,000
Increase in value			12,000
Less: improvements			(4,250)
Added value			7,750

In the above example, the estimated value of the property after improvements far outweighs the cost of the improvements themselves, giving a 'profit' of £7,750. The example assumes that the original state of the internal and external decoration etc. was bad enough to justify the expense, so that the improvements had a big enough impact to dramatically increase the final selling price. Had the property not been poorly decorated, and the original kitchen and front door were adequate, the picture would have been different. The value would have barely increased (if at all) so the improvements would not have passed the value to cost ratio test.

IMPROVEMENTS

When determining which individual improvements justify their cost and which do not, it helps to list the projects under review, estimate their price, then gauge the impact of each improvement, maybe by marking out of 10. This gives a clear order of importance, enabling easy identification and elimination of those improvements which have a high cost but low impact.

It may be that the property has been on the market for some time but has not achieved a sale, prompting the vendor to wonder whether certain improvements might increase the chance of finding a buyer. There is no reason why improvements should not be undertaken whilst a property is on the market, and some people do this so as not to miss any buyers who are looking for property during the time the improvements are being carried out. However, applicants who view a property in mid-repair and are not impressed are unlikely to make a further arrangement to view once the work is completed.

This is not a hard and fast rule, however, and there are exceptions like the case of a couple who bought a bungalow in Bristol which needed substantial modernisation. There was no kitchen to speak of, the floor in one of the rooms had to be sealed against damp, the interior needed complete redecoration and the garden was a mess. The couple bought the property for a good price in view of the considerable improvements required and set about getting the work done. Six months later when they came to sell the property, the first person who viewed it was a lady who had seen it before the alterations. At that time she liked it very much, but being quite elderly had not wanted the hassle of engaging builders and decorators. However, once the improvements had been carried out the property became a viable proposition and, happy to accept that the work had greatly increased the bungalow's value, she subsequently bought it. The couple who upgraded the property, came out of the deal with a 10% profit after costs, the buyer eventually got the property she wanted, so everyone was happy.

Sometimes when a property comes back on the market once improvements have been carried out it generates interest from people who viewed it before the work, as well as applicants who have only just started looking at property and are not aware of the property's original condition.

When deciding to carry out improvements to a property which has already been on the market for some time, the vendor may, after the improvements have been completed, wish to put the property under the instruction of a different agent who will see (and promote) the property with a fresh eye. Some agents have a problem accepting how much certain improvements can increase a property's value, and would rather promote a spotless bargain which they can sell quickly, instead of working hard to secure a higher selling price which an improved property's new status is capable of achieving. An extra £1,000 is a lot of money to the vendor, but the agent's 2% commission on this amount is only £20. If changing agents, be sure to read the small print in the original agent's Agreement since you may have to pay their fee if you sell through another agent within, say, six months of removing the property from their books.

Internal redecorating

In cases where a property is in dire need of revamping, maybe an inherited property which has been empty for some time, there may be just cause for complete internal redecoration, but this need not be as costly as one might imagine. Assuming the condition of the property is basically sound i.e. the walls and woodwork are in good condition, and basic maintenance has not been badly neglected, a new coat of plain paint right through will transform a badly decorated property into a 'clean slate' for the next owner. By redecorating, you will almost certainly increase the selling price, and stand a better chance of finding a buyer quickly.

Internal decoration probably has the biggest effect of all on a prospective buyer, so it pays to take an objective look to see if it can be improved. In most cases a new coat of paint is enough to immediately 'lift' a room. As an example of what paint can do, I once inherited a miserable kitchen which had a mis-match of brown units and tired wallpaper. By painting the walls a cheerful yellow and giving the units several coats of white gloss, the room became bright and the units looked as though they matched. Any room which feels dark and dingy can easily be transformed with masses of paint at a relatively low cost.

As another example of the effectiveness of paint, a neighbour once told of a small terraced house which she inherited from an aged aunt. The decision to sell the house was made and since it was well situated in a busy town a quick sale was anticipated. However, although many people viewed the property, it failed to attract a buyer. After a visit to the house to discuss the situation with the selling agents, the owner decided some cheap internal decoration would be well worth the expense and enlisted the services of a local painter and decorator. A complete transformation with magnolia painted walls and white woodwork took less than a week, and the house then sold to the first person who viewed it.

In deliberating over the value of internal redecoration we have so far only looked at repainting, whereas some vendors may be faced with the prospect of stripping existing wallpaper which is both labour intensive and time consuming. Before taking this step, bear in mind that the state of the wall underneath the paper might not be quite what it appears and this could be the very reason it was papered in the first place. Whilst hanging wallpaper is for some experienced DIY'ers quicker than painting, the cost is usually higher, so painting over the existing paper might be a cheaper option, assuming the texture and finish are suitable. As a final point, whilst the extensive choice of wallpaper patterns, textures and colours gives great scope for imaginative decorating and individual style, if it is not to the taste of a prospective buyer he is then faced with the unattractive prospect of stripping it off again.

External redecorating

Whilst redecorating internally can be relatively cheap and is something the vendor can often do himself, external redecoration is another story altogether and unless the property is single story will involve the use of ladders and/or scaffolding. Given this, the vendor may not be able to do the work himself and will incur the cost of employing someone to do it for him, as well as the cost of materials. Properties which have not been rendered, stone-washed or otherwise painted will have minimum redecorating requirements; probably only windows and doors, but a fashion for painting the fabric of buildings has left many homeowners with the recurring expense of repainting every so often.

One of the problems when painting external woodwork and plaster is the weather. Rain stops work instantly and can be disastrous if it suddenly pours onto a newly glossed window or door, whereas bright sunshine makes painting light colours a painful experience similar to snow-blindness. Weather which is too hot means that the paint does not dry effectively; too cold and the decorator might not turn up!

Having said all that, a new coat of paint can do wonders for the appearance of a property if it really needs it, and if the vendor can do the work himself to avoid labour costs, it may be worth considering as an improvement which could add not only to the value but also the saleability of the property. However, if the existing decoration is not too bad, it probably would not be cost effective to go to the expense of repainting, which can run into thousands of pounds.

Major repairs

If redecorating is not enough, and substantial repairs are envisaged, care must be taken not to spend money which cannot be recouped from the resulting sale price. Any improvements, repairs or alterations must justify their cost, either by increasing the value of the property, or improving on its saleability by making it appeal to a wider audience than just builders or DIY enthusiasts. If the property is in decay, repairing and redecorating will probably recoup the outlay, since the days when buyers were falling over themselves to invest in run down properties to sell for a profit after a lick of paint are long gone, and the vendor of a property in need of major repairs is unlikely to find a buyer at all unless he is prepared to sell at a low price.

The trick is to decide wisely which repairs are necessary and which are not, so when considering undertaking major repairs the vendor will need to decide:

1.Which repairs are urgent?

If a particular defect is likely to cause further damage if left uncorrected, then this will obviously be a priority. You do not want the relatively simple task of repairing a leaking window to escalate into problems of rotten timbers and damaged decoration when rainwater starts to run down the wall. On the other hand, you do not want to spend a great deal of money replacing a run-down garage if the addition of a such a building will not raise the value of the property significantly to cover the cost of installation.

2.Which repairs need to be carried out before selling?

The vendor may need to prioritise those repairs which need to be done before the property is placed on the market. But If you want to put the property up for sale without delay, it may not be necessary to wait until all repairs have been finalised before instructing agents to begin marketing. Some repairs (like re-pointing a chimney) will not affect viewing appointments, although having builders working on site during a viewing appointment is not such a good idea, but some other repairs cause considerable mess and upheaval which will hinder your efforts to show the property in an appealing light. To the inexperienced eye some damage looks more serious than it is, when the actual cost and severity of the repair may be much less than expected, whilst at the opposite end of the scale an apparently simple repair to a small area of damp can result in the removal of great chunks of plaster and will necessitate redecoration after the work has been completed.

TOP TIP
When getting quotes for repairs, ask how much disruption will be involved and clarify exactly how long the job will take.

---

3. Which repairs will affect a valuation or survey?

Speak to estate agents, many of whom will be able to recount their own experiences of properties which have been difficult to sell because of one defect or another. Also, speak to a surveyor (you will find them listed in the telephone directory), explaining that you are about to place your property on the market and are concerned that, for example, the state of the roof could reflect badly in a valuation or survey. The surveyor should be able to advise which roof problems are serious and which are not – a few missing roof tiles will not feature highly in a report, whereas rotting roof timbers will be of greater concern. This will enable you to determine whether the repair is really necessary to 'pass' a surveyor's inspection.

4. How much will the repairs cost?

Most of us will be directed by our bank balance when deciding the amount of work we can afford to undertake, so vendors will need to get several quotes and then decide whether or not they can afford to do the work. Ascertaining the cost of each repair will also enable the vendor to prioritise, and if a repair is excluded on grounds of cost, the vendor at least has up-do-date quotes to hand to give a prospective buyer a realistic idea of how much the work will cost. A buyer will naturally try to negotiate the selling price down to reflect any work necessary to bring the property up to scratch, but at least the negotiations will be fair if the vendor can produce evidence of anticipated costs, instead of being unable to argue against reducing the price by thousands of pounds for a repair which would actually cost less than a few hundred.

Once you have quotes for the repair costs, you will be in a position to decide whether it is best to:

- get an expensive fault rectified, if it affects the saleability and/or sale price; or
- attend to smaller defects that give the property an overall impression of poor maintenance.

5. Effect of repairs on selling price

The number one priority for most vendors is achieving the highest possible selling price, so the extent to which outstanding repairs reflect on the selling price attainable will be a major factor in deciding whether or not they are done. It is easy to assume the selling price of a property in need of repair can be set at the market value of a similar property in good repair less deductions to cover the cost of necessary work. In reality however, many other factors influence the selling price of such a property, on top of the cost of repairs, and for properties with structural damage or in need of major repairs or renovations, buyers demand a far keener price reduction.

Negotiations will take into account the element of risk involved, real or imagined, in buying a property which will require significant financial outlay on top of the purchase price. The buyer may express his concern that further defects could be uncovered once work commences, especially if he is not willing to go to the expense of a full survey. The vendor could offer to pay for the survey to set his prospective buyer's mind at rest, but should be aware that they can cost several hundred pounds, and there is no guarantee the sale will proceed, even if the survey is favourable.

If the buyer is a builder (and in the case of severely run down properties this could be the only type of buyer the property attracts) he will naturally be looking to make a profit on the resale. After all he has to eat too! Whilst the builder may appear to submit a very low offer, he has to allow for the cost of funding the project on top of the cost of repairs. If the property is empty for some time until resold, the builder will either loose interest on his own funds or incurr interest payments to a lender.

A buyer who is able to buy property which falls outside the normal channels of funding has the vendor of the property over a financial barrel. Both buyer and vendor know that the chances of a further offer arising, let alone a higher one, are doubtful.

Anyone who has ever experienced building work in the home will appreciate the inconvenience it causes. Dust on every surface, even in rooms where there is no work going on, and banging and hammering which seem to be part of any repair job sends you either mad or deaf. The buyer will therefore be considering the 'price' of such upheaval and will want to be compensated, since his only alternative, if he can afford it, is not to live in the property whilst the work is being completed, in which case he will incur additional living expenses, either in rent or else by delaying his own sale whilst purchasing the property with a bridging loan. Any such additional costs incurred by the buyer will be built into his financial equation when arriving at a price he is willing to offer.

The aesthetic appeal of a property is marred by neglect. This is an obvious point, but reflects very highly on the price a property can command. A pretty cottage which appeals to a large audience will reach a far higher price than its size and location justifies, because people really want it. Buyers often buy simply because the 'feel' of a place is right, or something about it appeals to them over all the others they have seen. A neglected property is unlikely to inspire a buyer into thinking 'I must have it, and I am prepared to pay however much it takes (within reason) to get it'.

6. Effect of repairs on saleability

Whether or not a property appeals to a wide market will often determine whether or not it sells quickly. It is true to say that the vendor only needs to attract one keen buyer to secure a sale, but finding the right buyer in a small market can be a problem. Sometimes the selling agents have difficulty encouraging potential buyers to even look at properties which require repair or renovation, let alone secure a sale on them. Applicants who register with estate agents are usually asked a series of questions about the type of property they are looking for to enable to agent to send them details of only those properties which will be of interest. One of the questions the agents frequently ask is whether or not the applicant will consider taking on a property in need of repair. The applicant will, at this stage, have no idea what type of repairs the agent is referring to, the extent of work involved or the type of property, but will often imagine the most depressing of pictures, fearing a property which is severely run down. They will consequently reply that they will not consider buying a property in need of repair, thereby dismissing them all without even having seen the agent's details on which to base such a rejection. In this way the agent's marketing reaches a limited number of potential buyers.

DID YOU KNOW?   *An attractive property in need of repair and renovation often fits the requirement of a successful auction and could sell more quickly through an auction than on the open market.*

Sometimes a potential buyer finds he has to withdraw from the purchase of a property in need of repair once the survey or valuation report is received. When a surveyor is instructed to carry out a valuation report or survey, part of the reason for obtaining the report is to safeguard the lender against funding more than a property is actually worth in its present condition, which would make the loan unsecured. This being so, the result of a valuation or survey will not only decide a property's value, but will also dictate the type of buyer who will be able to fund the purchase. The vendor of a property in need of costly repairs may find a buyer who is prepared to carry out the repairs, but if the valuation or survey recommends the lender limits funding because of major defects, the buyer may not be able to raise sufficient funds to cover the purchase price and the cost of repairs. The purchase price may be acceptable to the buyer because he appreciates the property's value will be increased once the repairs have been carried out, but the lender will only fund the proportion of the purchase price which a surveyor suggests is it's value <u>at that time</u>. Building societies and other financial institutions do not base their lending criteria on a property's potential worth, but rather on its market value at the time of purchase.

DID YOU KNOW?   *Necessary repairs may need to be done between exchange and completion at the insistance of the buyer's lender.*

In other words, if the property does not come under the normal lending criteria, the market for such a property is limited to those buyers who are able to personally fund a high proportion of the purchase price from their own funds, and the number of buyers who can afford to do this is small.

Properties in need of major renovations do sometimes sell quickly because they are attractively priced and inspire buyers into imagining what they will be like once the renovations are completed. At the other end of the scale, properties which are in pristine condition also tend to sell quickly because of their aesthetic appeal. It is those properties which fall in between these two categories which take longer than usual to sell, particularly if the condition leans towards being 'in need of updating and improvement', in other words rather tatty and unappealing, but not priced to inspire.

Grants

Some improvements or repairs may be eligible for grant aid through the Local Council. The type of grants available vary according to area and are usually subject to some form of means testing. A Renovation Grant applies mainly to 'raising the standard' of the property, for example installing a bathroom where previously there was none, and is available for properties built or converted over 10 years ago.

Present rules stipulate that grant monies must be repaid if the property is sold within three years, but the amount of repayment is proportionately reduced over the three year period. So, if the vendor sells after three years he will not need to repay any of the grant, but if he sells within 18 months he will need to repay half of it. Even for the vendor who sells immediately, the grant system might still be financially worthwhile (assuming the cost of repairs increases the selling price), because it would probably be a cheaper way of raising funds than borrowing through a bank or other lender who will charge interest.

Be sure to retain any documents relating to grants since you may need to present these to your buyer's solicitor.

Additions and alterations

Many people don't present their property in its best light because they do not want to spend money on anything which will be left behind as part of the fixtures and fittings. This is a relevant point. However, it can be worth making a few minor adjustments to what you already have in order to make the property look better and so appeal to more buyers. It is very difficult to categorise those things which you probably WILL get your money back on, and those which you WONT, but generally speaking any custom made luxury is unlikely to be worth the outlay, whilst 'impact improvements' like internal or external 'face lifts' usually recoup their cost and make a property easier to sell. When considering new installations, the vendor needs to bear in mind that few people are prepared to pay thousands of pounds for a second hand kitchen or fitted wardrobes (and any new purchases you make will be second hand to a buyer), so the costs need to be balanced very carefully against the anticipated increase in selling price.

Below are some alterations and additions which can improve the impression of a property without costing a small fortune, and vendors may find that one or two alterations make a difference to the chances of finding a buyer, although none of them, certainly when taken individually, are likely to dramatically increase the final selling price.

• Flooring

The range of floor coverings available ensures that there is something for every home and every pocket. Carpets are probably the most popular form of floor covering and come in every variation from cheap and cheerful coir matting, to the best Wilton or Axminster. In between these there is a whole range of carpets in hundreds of different colours, styles and standards of quality.

> **TOP TIP**
>
> Roll ends of carpet can appear to be good value, but check the price against the usual 'cut to measure' price to make sure you really are getting a good deal. Also, many retailers include fitting and delivery with cut to measure orders but do not do so with roll end sales, so be prepared to either fit it yourself or employ a carpet fitter.

It may not be necessary to go to the expense of buying new carpets to brighten up a room. Sometimes perfectly good tiles or wood flooring can be found under old carpet, and if the floorboards are sound these can be stained, painted and even, if you are artistic and patient, stencilled. Many DIY stores hire sanding machines designed specifically for preparing wooden floors for exposure to paint or varnish. This is a relatively cheap way of getting round the expense of replacing old carpet, but it is time consuming and hard work.

Ordinarily a good quality carpet is a sound investment and the cheaper versions can turn out to be a false economy. However, when replacing carpet for the purposes of selling a property it does not make economic sense to spend a great deal of money for top quality which will probably be left behind as part of the fixtures and fittings. If replacing carpet as an improvement simply to attract a buyer, it is far more sensible to opt for an economy carpet which looks just as good. Usually the most hard-wearing carpet is the most expensive and whilst it may not be worth buying the very best, vendors should beware of cheap carpet which will look sorry for itself in a matter of weeks, especially if used inappropriately, i.e. bathroom carpet in a hall

Vinyl floor coverings have improved beyond all recognition in recent years. Gone are the old thin vinyls which curled at the edges and were cold and dull, and in come the much improved versions which do a very good impression of expensive woodblock or parquet flooring at a fraction of the cost.

• Lighting

All too often lighting comes a long way down on the list or priorities in the original planning of a room, and the positioning and number of electrical fitments and sockets do not allow much scope to create intimate pools of light instead of a blanket of purely functional illumination. However, a little thought and imagination can improve lighting dramatically without any need for re-wiring or expensive new fitments. If, having considered where lighting should be, you find that the positioning of the sockets is restrictive, a longer replacement lead will enable existing table lamps etc. to be positioned almost anywhere. Pelmet lights are slim and easy to hide and, since they can be powered from a normal plug and socket arrangement, can be hidden to give concealed lighting effects. If the leads are passed behind furniture or under carpet they will not be noticeable and this opens up a whole new avenue of lighting.

Lampshades and/or bases can be painted (using appropriate paint) as a very cheap way of creating a co-ordinated effect with furniture and decoration, and any additional lights purchased, so long as they are not included in the sale price, can be taken with you.

Lighting outside the front of a property gives a good first impression and makes access to the property on a dark night easier than stumbling up a dark path or steps. There are many decorative 'lantern' style external lights, but make sure they are rain proof and do not have loose fitments or glass which can let in water.

• Soft Furnishings

Whether or not the vendor decides to leave curtains as part of the fixtures and fittings of the sale is up to him. Many vendors assume that they have to leave curtains when actually this is not the case, and in any event the buyer might not want them. If the vendor decides to update his curtains for the purposes of improving the look of the rooms to attract a buyer, he does not necessarily have to leave the new curtains as part of the sale, so assuming they are suitable for his next property he can taken them with him. The Fixtures Fittings and Contents form which the vendor will be required to complete, will ask him to specify in which rooms curtains will be left.

Net curtains can be expensive and unnecessary from an aesthetic point of view, unless they are used to block an unattractive outlook or to improve the appearance of the window by covering it up. However, there are a multitude of different styles available and introducing or replacing nets might be a cheaper alternative to replacing the actual curtains when attempting to 'pretty up' a window. One of the benefits of net curtains is that, if they are bright white, they make the window itself bright even on a dull day. Where nets are discoloured, badly fitting or just plain tatty, they are probably best removed and the window left without any if the vendor decides not to replace them. From the outside especially, grubby nets are extremely unappealing and very obvious.

Other soft furnishings do not usually form part of the fixtures, fittings or contents which the vendor is expected to leave behind, so any additions or replacements will remain the possessions of the vendor after the sale. Making rather than buying replacement soft furnishings to cheer up a room might be an option for vendors who are handy with a needle, but this is not necessarily any cheaper than buying.

Since beds are such a prominent feature in bedrooms, the soft furnishings used for quilt covers or bedspreads are obviously a big part of the impact given when entering the bedroom on a viewing. New quilt covers can be purchased relatively cheaply and in a huge range of styles and colours, so the cost of buying material rarely makes running up your own cost effective.

• Plants

Plants make a big difference to a room and an interesting foliage display can be a cheap way of bringing interest to a bare area. A few plants in a bathroom, for example, bring light relief and colour when positioned against plain tiling, and create atmosphere where previously there was none. The range of plants is extensive, although some can be extremely expensive. Others, however, bring a splash of colour far more cheaply than a vase of fresh flowers, have the same welcoming effect and will last for more than one viewing. Assuming, that is, they are looked after properly. Some people serve a death sentence on a plant as soon as they buy it, usually because of over zealous watering, but most garden centres or flower shops have qualified staff who will be able to advise on the most suitable plant for a particular position, i.e. whether it will survive best in light or shade, in a warm position or best kept cool, so it is always advisable to check the suitability of plants before buying them.

TOP TIP
Indoor plants attract dust, so giving the leaves a wipe gives the plant renewed colour and shine. Specialist plant products are available for leaf cleaning, or alternatively damp cotton wool works well.

• Gardens

Turning to plants outside the property, it is probably not cost effective to go to the expense of acquiring plants and shrubs to attract a buyer. Whether or not a well stocked garden is a selling point will depend on the buyer and what he is looking for, and for some buyers the prospect of keeping a complicated garden well tended will be seen as a disadvantage when viewing. For gardens which are completely wild, having the area dug over and turfed could be a worthwhile investment, particularly if the project is small enough to be tackled by the vendor himself and does not necessitate hiring machinery for preparation of the ground. When considering the cost of laying a new lawn, grass seed is cheaper than turf (which comes in pre-cut sections or 1ft x 1m usually), but turf gives an instant effect. The ground needs to be prepared well for both methods, particularly so with seed when you will need to keep off the area until the grass appears.

Bedding plants give an instant splash of colour to a dull patch of garden, but are expensive if the area to be filled is large. A patio might be worth the expense of a few colourful plants and these do not need be put into expensive containers when large plastic plant pots can be just as effective and cost much less.

TOP TIP

Plants on a patio can turn an austere block of concrete into a charming sitting/eating place, especially if garden furniture is positioned to show the area is enjoyed as such.

At the front of the property, plants create a cheerful welcome to any potential buyers who come to view it. Although as already mentioned bedding plants are expensive, a few grouped together will make an instant improvement to a dull entrance, particularly if positioned near the building itself. Hanging baskets and tubs give an instant lift and, unless specified as part of the contents, need not be left by the vendor on completion of the sale. Hanging baskets are traditionally used in spring and summer, but they can be planted for winter colour (with winter flowering pansies for example) if the positioning is suitable.

Employing a landscape gardener will be expensive, but in the rare instance where the garden represents a large proportion of the property's asking price it might be worth the expense i.e. a house being sold with 2 acres of 'grounds' will command a higher selling price than a house sold with 2 acres of rough ground. Taking this option would require a good deal of financial outlay and care would be needed to ascertain the costs involved in ground clearance, re-planting etc. compared to the anticipated increase in selling price, to make sure such an outlay is cost effective.

Clearing rough ground is back-breaking work, but if replanting or grassing is not an option which appears cost effective or affordable, simply clearing flower beds of weeds and raking up dead leaves will make a big difference at no cost at all.

TOP TIP
In small gardens, low plants make the area seem bigger.

• Replacement kitchens

The kitchen is undoubtedly one of the most important rooms in a property, and the huge market in new kitchens only goes to show how impressed we are by fitted units which offer practical cooking arrangements together with luxurious good looks.

A replacement kitchen is often the most expensive addition to the home and as such an attractive kitchen is a selling point that can add to the value of a property. Having said that, an imaginative kitchen which does not cost the earth can have the same positive effect on prospective buyers as one which has been purchased at great cost. Some of the most attractive kitchens are a combination of units and dressers, giving a warmer and more friendly look than a pre-planned arrangement of units covering every wall. Fitted kitchens are very expensive and it can often be a cheaper option to buy free standing items of furniture rather than fitted units. The main advantages of fitted kitchens is that they come in a style to suit every taste, in a wide range of prices and can make the most of a very small or awkward area.

Under normal circumstances, replacing an existing kitchen with new units is probably not a cost effective improvement, and it may be a wiser use of funds to improve on what is already there, rather than ripping out and starting again (see Chapter 3). If there is scope to add an item of furniture to the kitchen which would improve its look, maybe a different table or a dresser, this could make a difference to the appeal of the room and not leave the vendor out of pocket since such an item would not be a 'fixture' to be left behind on completion of the sale.

For a kitchen which is either in very poor shape or where there is no kitchen at all, installing a new kitchen could add not only to the purchase price of the property but may also increase its saleability. (An exception to this would be where the whole property is in need of renovation and is priced accordingly.) Whether or not installing a kitchen is cost effective to a particular property will depend to on how much is spent on the kitchen in relation to the resultant increase in selling price. It would not be wise to spend many thousands on a replacement kitchen in a property with a relatively low selling price because the proportionate increase would not cover the cost.

Whilst the style of an expensive kitchen will appeal to the vendor who chooses it, it may not be to the taste of the eventual buyer, this is one of the reasons many new home builders do not install kitchen units until a buyer makes an offer on the property. The builder then gives the buyer a selection of unit styles to make a selection from, so that the buyer gets a brand new kitchen of his choice.

TOP TIP

It is possible for a vendor to use his dilapidated kitchen as a selling point, by agreeing to install a new kitchen of the buyer's choice (from a selection falling within a certain price range, of course). The new kitchen would need to be installed after exchange of contracts to be sure that the sale was going ahead, and the arrangement would need to be clarified at the beginning of the transaction through the vendor's and buyer's solicitors to specify how many units are to be included etc.

As well as the services offered by carpenters and specialist kitchen builders, many general furniture stores and even DIY stores now sell kitchens of all types. Most of the cheapest are 'flat packed' and require assembly by the purchaser. Flat packed furniture has been around for many years, and the old advertising slogan used to be that a child of five years old could handle the assembly, to encourage the idea that anyone was capable of following the instructions. Unfortunately, the assembly did not turn out to be as simple as the advertising suggested, and the tongue in cheek joke for many people who bought these units and struggled to make something out of the box of obscure bits of wood and inappropriate fixings was that a child of five should be included in the price to decipher the instructions. Thankfully flat packed furniture and kitchen units have improved greatly over the years, and whilst it still takes considerable patience and time to assemble, at least the right nuts and bolts are included for the job and the instructions are fathomable without the help of children – just.

DID YOU KNOW? *Most kitchen cupboards have a similar carcass – only the doors are different.*

The price of a new kitchen rarely includes fitting, which can account for around a third of the cost of the kitchen itself. Even if the units come fully assembled, they still need to be fixed to the walls, and unless the new units are a straight 'out and in' replacement, there is likely to be some plumbing and electrical work involved. The cost of employing a plumber and/or electrician will need to be added to the cost of buying the kitchen to get a fair estimation of the total costs involved. Most kitchen retailers employ or subcontract a fitter who will give a quote for assembly and/or fitting, but the purchaser is not normally under obligation to employ the retailer's fitter, so other quotes should be obtained before assuming the quote is competitive.

The vendor who feels his kitchen is letting down his property in the eyes of prospective purchasers may not necessarily need to replace the whole kitchen in order to see an improvement. Replacing the sink or installing new worktops can instantly update an old kitchen, as can a coat of paint on the walls or even painting the units themselves if they are suitable.

Replacing 'white goods' like the fridge or cooker is not usually necessary, even if the buyer is moving from a property where the appliances are integral and so being including in his sale price. The replacements will still be second hand to the buyer, and some people do bring their own appliances, so new ones would be superfluous. It would be far better, rather than replacing appliances before securing a sale, to use the possible inclusion of new appliances as a bargaining tool when negotiating the selling price. You could say for example that you are willing to include certain new appliances if your sale price is met, or alternatively that you will accept the buyer's lower purchase offer without inclusion of the said appliances.

If you intend taking new appliances with you and not including them as part of the selling price, they may not be suitable in your new home or may be superfluous if the previous owner has included them in his selling price.

> **TOP TIP**
> Many stores offer a free kitchen planning service, giving the
> customer the benefit of their expertise to determine the best use of
> available space. The store usually supplies the customer with a
> final plan and quotation which the customer can then utilise to
> obtain estimates from other retailers for the same goods to make
> sure the price is competitive.

• Bathroom renovations

The cost of bathroom suites varies enormously, and whilst you can
spend a small fortune at the luxury end of the market, it is perfectly
possible to buy a new suite for a few hundred pounds or less. Given
the impact the suite has on the appearance of a bathroom because
the sheer size of the items dominate the room, it can be cost effective
to replace a bathroom suite if the existing one is in a bad condition.
The move away from dark coloured suites has meant that those
remaining in use now are rather dated and old fashioned, but if such
a bathroom suite is in good condition it might be a better use of funds
to 'pretty up' the rest of the room with new towels, shower curtain or
window blind, rather than replacing the suite. Popular modern
colours are light pastels and timeless white, though curiously there is
sometimes an extra charge for a white suite.

When replacing an old suite there will be some plumbing involved,
but if the positioning of the new items is the same as the existing
ones, i.e. a straight out and in job, this will be kept to a minimum. If
the intention is to add to the suite (maybe with a bidet or double sink
arrangement) or to alter the positioning of the items, it would be
advisable to obtain quotes for the plumbing work involved before
purchasing the additions as this can be expensive and could make the
project unworkable.

Increasingly showers are becoming part of the modern bathroom, but installation can be expensive both from the cost of electrical work involved and for purchase of the shower unit itself. Shower fitments which take water directly from bath taps are not generally considered worth promoting as a selling point because they have been updated by units which heat the water independently from the tank as it is needed. These modern showers are vastly superior, but whilst they vary enormously in price, even the cheapest is an expensive addition.

If there is room in the bathroom for a shower cubical, or if the position of the bath itself is suitable for mounting a shower fitment over, it might be more sensible for the vendor to bring the suitability of installing a shower to the attention of a prospective buyer without going to the expense of actually installing one. If the buyer likes the property well enough to consider buying it, it is unlikely that the absence of a shower would dissuade him from proceeding with the purchase

---

TOP TIP

When considering the installation of a shower unit, check the cost of plumbing and wiring as this can be more expensive than the shower unit itself.

Of course it may be that the bathroom suite itself is in a good condition but the room decoration is poor. This is not a problem when the decoration is either wallpaper or paint, and redecorating a comparatively small area like a bathroom should not present too many difficulties. However, many bathrooms have extensive wall tiling, which can make the scope for re-decorating seem very limited unless the existing tiles are either removed or replaced; an expensive and time consuming project. Re-tiling is not easy, as anyone who has tried it will testify, and removing tiles to expose a suitable surface for paint or paper will involve a great deal of work, especially since the exposed wall is likely to need a considerable amount of preparation. Happily there is a cheap and cheerful way of giving tiling a new lease of life for a minimum amount of work and expenditure, because it is possible to give the whole bathroom a facelift by changing the colour of old tiles with paint, without going to the expense of replacing them.

The tiles will need to be thoroughly cleaned and prepared before they can be painted. Certain paints work better than others, and a good decorating supplier will be able to advise which products are most suitable to ensure a good final result. Depending on the chosen style, the tiles could either be painted uniformly, or alternatively some of them could be painted to create a pattern, a border or as decoration around a mirror for example. The grouting on a tiled wall can be painted along with the tiles, and the sealant around baths and basins designed to stop water penetration can be renewed to give a clean finish.

Medicine and other bathroom cabinets, along with shower curtains and window blinds, are often included in the sale price. However, if replacement of such is all that is needed to cheer up a bathroom, but the vendor does not want to go to the expense of new purchases which will be left behind, they need not be included unless specified on the vendor's Fixtures Fittings and Contents list.

Ensuite facilities are now so common as to have become a requirement for many buyers, so much so that some people will only view properties which have ensuite facilities to the main bedroom at least. If a property has sufficient room for ensuite facilities (and an ensuite bath/shower room requires a surprisingly small amount of space) it might be worth the vendor asking his selling agent to include a footnote on the property details to the effect that there is sufficient room for the facilities, to avoid the details not going to those people who list ensuite facilities as a requirement.

The high cost of installing an ensuite bath or shower room means it is not a cost effective improvement in most cases. The relatively small cost of the fitments can lead one to the hasty conclusion that ensuite facilities would add sufficiently to the value of a property, justifying the cost of installation. However, the fitments will probably account for only a small percentage of the actual costs since there is plumbing and electrics to be considered and also the cost of building work to separate an area into the ensuite room. Add to that new floor covering, decorating and items like lighting, and the project quickly becomes a major expense. Another factor which can cause problems and additional expense is the provision of adequate ventilation, which is a requirement of Building Regulations.

DID YOU KNOW?   *Building regulations approval may be required when installing or altering the position of a WC, bath etc., or where there is new drainage or plumbing.*

Cloakrooms and additional WC's have also become very popular and these are imaginatively squeezed into the smallest of spaces under stairs and into rooms no bigger than a cupboard. Expenses similar to installing ensuite facilities will be incurred in addition to the actual WC fitments, and these will need to be worked into the overall budget to ascertain whether or not a cloakroom/WC is a cost effective addition.

Consents
Many additions and improvements need approval or permission from the local authority, and if the correct procedures are not followed the authority has the power to insist on remedial work or, in the case of new building work, demolition. This is expensive but, happily, avoidable. Be warned, the vendor who comes to sell his property without the necessary clearance documentation will face serious problems.

DID YOU KNOW? *It is not uncommon for a property sale to abort when a survey reveals that the vendor did not have planning permission or building regulation approval for work done at the property.*

It would be impossible to fully detail the working practices of different authorities up and down the country since they may have differing procedures and requirements, so a vendor who is considering any building work whatsoever would be best advised to check with the local authority to find out if permission or approval is required and, if so, what steps are needed to obtain it.

Many people confuse planning permission with building regulations approval (known in Scotland as a building control warrant), assuming they are the same thing. In fact they cover two distinct areas of legislation, and although some building projects may need both planning permission and building regulations approval, obtaining one does not automatically guarantee the other. When both are required, and given that planning permission may demand changes in design, it is sometimes better to obtain planning permission before preparing the detailed information needed to obtain building regulations approval.

Planning permission
Primary concern:– To decide whether a particular building or development is suited to the intended site and is in the public interest.

The planning department is generally concerned with the appearance of property and it's use, and controls can be decided by local policy as much as detailed regulation. Councils are unable to please all of the people all of the time, since they must use planning controls to protect the character and amenities of their area whilst still giving individuals reasonable freedom to alter their property. As a general rule, any addition or change which alters or affects the external appearance of a property may need planning permission, from minor additions like a satellite television aerial through to major building extensions. If permission is not granted, you may in retrospect need to carry out remedial work or even face the prospect of enforced demolition.

DID YOU KNOW? *Some councils issue design guides to assist in the designing of a building or extension.*

When considering a building project, you will firstly need to find out if planning permission is necessary. The way to do this is to contact the planning department of your local council and it is essential that you do this before starting any work.

As general guidance only, you <u>will</u> need planning permission if:

- The property is to be divided into separate dwellings.
- The property is to be divided to provide commercial or business accommodation.
- A caravan is to be placed in the grounds for use as a dwelling.
- You want to erect something which is contrary to the building's original planning permission.
- The work could obstruct the view of road users or requires the provision of, or extension of, access to a major road.

As a general rule planning permission <u>will not</u> be required for:

1. Extensions or additions, including conservatories, sun lounges and loft conversions. UNLESS:
   - The extension is closer to the highway (this includes the pavement) than the original building. The exception to this is if there is at least 20 meters between the finished extension and the highway.

- The extension would make the land around the original building more than half covered by additions or buildings.
- The extension is over 15% or 70 cubic meters greater than the original building (10% or 50 cubic meters in some areas). 115 cubic meters is the maximum.
- The extension exceeds the height of the roof.
- The extension is over 4 meters high.

DID YOU KNOW? *Most windows and skylights do not need planning permission, but bay windows are treated as extensions.*

2. Detached buildings on surrounding land, i.e. a greenhouse, shed, kennel or garage. UNLESS:

- The new building is closer to the highway (including pavement) than the original building. The exception to this is if there is at least 20 meters between the finished extension and the highway.
- The new building would make the land around the original building more than half covered by additions or buildings.
- The new building is not for domestic use.
- The new building will be more than 3 meters high (4 with a ridged roof).
- The new building will be storing heating oil with a capacity of more than 3,500 litres.
- The new building will be storing LPG gas.

3. Addition of a porch, UNLESS:

- The external measurements of the porch exceed 3 square meters, is more than 3 meters high or has less than 2 meters between it and a road.

4. Erection of a wall, fence or gate, UNLESS:

    • The building is listed.
    • The wall, fence or gate will be more than 2 meters high, or more than 1 meter high if next to a road.

5. Laying of a patio, hardstanding, path or driveway, UNLESS:

    • The surface is for commercial use.

6. Addition of an aerial or satellite dish, UNLESS:

    • It measures more than 70 centimetres in dimension (45 centimetres if attached to a chimney).
    • It is higher than the roof or chimney on which it is fixed.
    • It is in addition to an existing antenna.

7. Decoration, repairs, maintenance or demolition, UNLESS:

    • The building is listed.
    • The building to be demolished is larger than 50 cubic meters.

Applying for planning permission

Having ascertained that the building or alterations does require planning permission through discussions with the local authority, it

TOP TIP

If, having made verbal enquiries to the council, it appears that the proposal will not require planning permission, it is advisable to get their written confirmation of this to safeguard against a future dispute.

will be necessary to complete the appropriate application form(s) and submit the required fee in order for the proposal to be processed. Before completing forms and writing out cheques for fees, it might be useful to discuss the proposal with the local authority to see if the application is of something which they know is likely to be refused. You can then decide whether making the application is worthwhile.

You may decide to make an outline application first to obtain permission in principle before going to the trouble of preparing detailed drawings or plans, although these will be required later for a full application. The council will advise what drawings are needed, and these will need to be submitted with the forms and fee.

The council will acknowledge receipt of the application (usually within a few days) and will then place it on the planning register so that it is open to inspection by members of the public. They may also contact your neighbours or put up a site notice to ascertain local opinion and may advertise the proposals in the local press.

DID YOU KNOW? *If the building proposal raises objections, you can usually have sight of these at the council offices or obtain copies.*

The proposals should either be approved or refused within around eight weeks, but the council may request your consent for an extension to this period.

Building regulations
Primary Concern:- **To ensure that the design, construction and use of a building is safe, is not a fire hazard, is damp proof and rain proof, and has adequate ventilation, access, heat insulation and toilet facilities.**

The job of the building control officer is to ensure that building work confirms to complex rules designed to ensure public and personal safety. He must satisfy himself that any alterations comply with minimum building specifications, that the building materials used are suitable and that the building method is satisfactory. Not every structural alteration will need building regulation approval, but if it transpires that it was needed after the work has been carried out, perfectly satisfactory work may need to be undone simply to prove that it was carried out according to regulations.

Obtaining building regulations approval

The first thing to do is ascertain whether the alteration actually needs approval or not, by contacting the local authority. Whilst there are exceptions which makes it imperative that local authority guidance is sought, a broad guide of which alterations or additions will require approval and those which will not, can be summarised into the following categories:

Required:
- All building work unless excluded under Schedule 2 of the Building Regulations.
- Loft conversions.
- Garage conversions to living accommodation.
- Internal alterations such as removing a wall to turn two rooms into one.
- Conversion from single dwelling into flats.
- Cavity wall insulation.
- Installation of gas, solid fuel or oil heating appliances.
- Installation of fittings which require new plumbing, i.e. WC.

Not required:
- Replacement windows.
- Car port.

- Conservatory.
- Porch.
- Minor repairs.
- Erection of a boundary wall.
- Installation of fittings, unless requiring new drainage or plumbing.

Having ascertained that building regulation approval is required, information about the addition or alteration will be required by the Authority, usually in the form of either a full plan or building notice.

DID YOU KNOW? *To ensure public safety, a licence from the Highway Authority must be obtained before scaffolding can be erected or a skip can be placed on the public highway (this includes pavements and grass verges as well as roads). A fee is payable for both a scaffolding or skip licence.*

The full plan can be drawn up by the vendor himself so long as it confirms to certain requirements, mainly that it is to a recognised scale, includes constructions notes and all major dimensions, and that proposed work is clearly distinguishable from the original building. If the vendor prefers not to prepare his own plan he can enlist the services of an architect or surveyor. The Authority is obligated to give a decision on a plan within five weeks, but this time restraint can sometimes force the Authority to reject the plan if they do not have sufficient information to hand by that time in order to pass it. It is possible to allow the Authority an extension by prior arrangement of up to two months from the date the plans are deposited with them. Once the plan has been checked and approved, the Authority will issue an Approval Notice. On completion of the work to the requirements of the regulations, a Completion Certificate can be obtained (see below).

Building notices can be submitted instead of a full plan, but will not be acceptable for all types of application. A site plan will probably be required and further details may be requested at a later date, and it is worth checking with the authority that they will issue a Completion Certificate under this procedure before deciding against a Full Plans submission. Submitting a building notice will generally save the vendor time, because there are no plans which require approval by the local authority. However because of this an Approval Notice will not be given, so the vendor or his builder will need to work closely with the building control officer to avoid potential problems or retrospective work requirements.

Fees

With both full plan and Building Notices, a fee will be payable to the Authority, the amount of which will depend on the type of work. Both procedures will demand a similar fee, the only difference being that it is payable in two instalments with a full plan (part on submission of the plan, part after the first inspection), whereas the fee covering Building Notices is paid in full after the first inspection.

Completion Certificate

It is important to indicate when obtaining building regulations approval that a Completion Certificate is required. This Certificate is the vendor's 'proof' that the building work has been carried out correctly in accordance with the requirements of building regulations, and is an important document when the property is being sold, since without it the standard of the work is questionable and the buyer's surveyor may have doubts that the building is sound. The Authority will only issue the Certificate when they are in receipt of all statutory notifications.

DID YOU KNOW? *A proposed change of access from a public road i.e., a new driveway, may require approval by the Highways Department.*

The title deeds of a house or flat will frequently contain strict conditions about the structure of the building and may rule out the possibility of certain additions or alterations. With a leasehold flat, for example, the landlord may refuse permission for the addition of a dividing wall. Although it is sometimes possible (at a cost) to get agreement to change these restrictions, the vendor should make sure that he has permission to implement the intended alterations before proceeding with the work.

When a vendor comes to sell his property, he can encounter lengthy delays and major headaches if he does not have the relevant documents to show that an improvement or addition has any necessary planning permission, building regulations approval, completion certificate and authority of the title. Even worse, the sale can be lost and/or the purchase price reduced.

In summary:
- Decide which improvements/repairs/alterations are cost effective.
- To be cost effective they need to add sufficiently to the property's value to at least recoup their cost.
- Decide which improvements/repairs/alterations are most likely to increase the saleability of the property.
- Approach the local authority to ascertain whether planning permission or building regulation approval is needed BEFORE embarking on any work.

VIEWINGS

Viewings are a crucial part of property selling. If no-one comes to view a property being sold there is little chance of selling it. No customers means no business, but the crucial part of selling a home is getting the right people to view, then turning those potential buyers into positive buyers. It seems simple enough, but how may viewings should a vendor expect to conduct before one of them results in a sale? This is difficult to answer. It will depend on the type of property, since some will have a wider market than others, and whether or not the property market is active at the time. It will also depend on whether the selling agent is active or passive, efficient or inefficient.

Vendors often imagine the effectiveness of their estate agent can be measured by the volume of viewings they receive. In most cases this is simply not true, and if a property is shown to a lot of potential buyers, none of whom show any positive interest, then the wrong people are viewing. Unfortunately for the selling agents, they cannot win in the eyes of the vendor. If they take the time to interview all applicants at length to ascertain what each applicant is looking for and so avoid arranging unsuitable viewings, the agents disappoint the vendor because the number of viewings they arrange is slimmed down. If on the other hand the agents send plenty of applicants to view the properties they are selling, regardless of suitability, then the vendors are justifiably irritated by the inconvenience of appointments which amount to nothing. When agents take a long time to achieve a sale they are accused of not working hard enough, but if they sell the property quickly the vendor wonders whether the property was marketed too cheaply.

So what is the agent to do? His job, if he is capable, is firstly to spread a marketing net wide enough to attract as many applicants as possible, then promote each property to all those applicants who might conceivably buy that type of property. However, in reality, some agents do not ascertain what an applicant is looking for and so arrange unsuitable viewings. This is very time consuming for applicants (who view unsuitable properties), for vendors (who show unsuitable applicants around their home) and for the agents themselves, who arrange the appointments. Some vendors will be happy with this arrangement because they hope a flood of viewings will eventually secure a sale, and there might be an element of wisdom in this because sometimes an applicant can be persuaded to buy a property which, before viewing, he might have thought was not suitable.

However, whilst it is time consuming for vendors to conduct unsuccessful viewings, it is important that agents do not slim down their viewing appointments so far that they miss a sale by not sending an applicant to view a particular property because they have assumed, wrongly, that they know fully what the applicant is looking for. This type of over confidence can lose the opportunity of securing a sale. Applicants can and do change their priorities between the time of registering as an applicant and the time of purchase, so agents should regularly consult with applicants to be aware of any new or differing requirements to avoid discounting properties which may in retrospect be suitable.

An applicant will eventually buy only one of the dozens of properties he views, so it follows that vendors can reasonably expect some unsuccessful viewings. But, if the vendor is conducting plenty of viewings without achieving a sale, or if he is not receiving viewings at all, he needs urgently to find out why this is so.

If a property is not attracting viewings it is easy to assume that the agents are at fault, but it may be that the property is priced too highly, especially if there are plenty of other properties on the market at that time of a comparable type but which are priced lower. If on the other hand a property is attracting plenty of viewings, but no-one is coming up with an offer, it may be that all the applicants rejecting the property for the same reason, in which case the vendor may be able to do something to rectify whatever is obstructing the sale. It probably won't be the price which is the problem, unless the condition of the property does not warrant it's price on closer inspection. It only takes one keen buyer to secure a sale, but if a property does not meet the requirements of the people who are viewing it, no matter how many of them there are, it will not sell.

Once a property attracts an applicant who is looking for that type of property and is sufficiently interested to make an appointment to view, the vendor is part way to securing an offer. Forgetting for a moment the complications of finance, buying positions and fine timing, at this stage the first thing a vendor needs is to find applicants who want to view his property. Once the appointment to view has been arranged, the property then has to impress sufficiently to prompt an offer, and for the best chance of a success it needs to be prepared and presented effectively (see Chapters 2 and 3).

TOP TIP

Make sure an applicant is able to park easily when arriving for a viewing, moving your own car elsewhere if necessary.

Successful retailers spend a great deal of time and money on presentation in an effort to promote their product favourably, and many aspects of effective presentation and sales can be learnt from observing high street retailers. An immediately apparent aspect of retail presentation and promotion is that not all retailers aim their product at the same section of the market. Supermarkets, for example, vary in the way they set out to attract customers, but most of them can be put into one of two groups; those who attract with quality products, good service and pleasant surroundings, and those who attract purely with low prices. The moral of this example is this: if you are marketing a product to sell very cheaply you don't need to go to much trouble with presentation, but if you don't want to compete on price, you will.

TOP TIP

During a viewing, your property is being "interviewed".
Ask yourself this - Would you attend an interview unprepared or inappropriately dressed? And if you did, would you expect to get the job? No, of course not, and what a waste of time the whole ordeal would have been.

The cause of many fruitless viewings used to be deceptive property details. Over-imaginative descriptions and clever photography gave an image which bore little resemblance to the actual building, and consequently applicants often found themselves viewing totally unsuitable properties. Agents operated under the theory that the best way to sell property was to arrange as many viewing appointments as possible, regardless of suitability, most of them inevitably doomed to failure, in the vague hope that a match between applicant and property was bound to occur eventually, if only by the law of averages. The principle of this seemed reasonable and was fairly successful at a time when the property market was flooded with eager buyers, but the practice is not recommended nowadays.

Thankfully, the Property Misdescription Act has gone some way to stamping out this practice and estate agents are required to refrain from embellishing their written property details with misleading information. This means that buyers who receive details of a property now have a very clear picture of what to expect from that property before they view it, and will consequently find the right property more quickly. All of which should aid the process of buying and selling.

Nowadays vendors can be fairly sure while conducting a viewing that their property fits reasonably well into the applicant's requirements. Of course applicants will see several similar properties before they decide which one to buy, but at least each property has as much chance as all the others on the applicants list, and is not the wrong size or type to begin with.

Making viewings easy

One of the great headaches suffered by estate agents arises when they try to contact a client to arrange a viewing appointment, but the client is nowhere to be found. In one case, a couple crossed several counties to post a note through the door of a property they wished to view because the agents could not contact the owner. Of course the agent conducting the sale should have been the one to post the note, but luckily for the vendor the purchasers were determined people and eventually bought the house. Other vendors might not be so lucky, so they should try to be easily contactable. If this is not always possible, vendors will need to check with the agents regularly to see if they have been trying to arrange a viewing, or risk losing the chance of a sale.

The heady days when every property had half a dozen willing buyers will probably never return, so bearing this in mind it is now necessary to accommodate viewing appointments whenever possible. This does not mean that vendors need to sit by the telephone waiting for it to ring, but they should nevertheless be willing to accept viewings at the convenience of applicants. It is dangerous to assume that applicants will fit in with the vendor's timetable if they are interested enough, and sales have been lost in cases where the vendor makes viewing arrangements difficult. True, a keen applicant may view at the vendor's convenience, but then again he might not, and with so many sellers competing for a handful of buyers, can you afford to take the gamble?

Agency conducted viewings

The vendor who trusts his agents implicitly may be willing to give them a key so that they can conduct viewings at any time when he is unavailable to do so himself. If you think this arrangement will suit you, it is worth arranging for the agent to conduct at least one viewing in your presence, so that you can see him 'in action' to make sure he is competent, and if he is, you will be able to pick up a few tips on technique for the occasions when you conduct viewings yourself. Agency viewings can be very convenient for vendors who are often unavailable, but it is important to ensure that the agent takes reasonable care with the keys, so vendors need to make sure their keys are never left lying around the office, tagged with the address. If entrusting the agent with keys, ask to see how they are stored – ideally they should be in a locked cabinet, indirectly identified by code, the code book stored away from the cabinet.

DID YOU KNOW? *Agents who conduct viewings on behalf of vendors often allow applicants to go from room to room unsupervised. If you want the agent to keep an eye on applicants whilst they are in your home be sure to insist on this, but do not assume that your wishes will always be adhered to.*

A big disadvantage of agency viewings is that as the vendor does not get the opportunity to make last minute preparations, this means the property needs to be permanently prepared for inspection, just in case, which is a nuisance for those who would normally go to work leaving beds unmade and breakfast dishes in the sink. Another major disadvantage is that the vendor is leaving the important job of 'selling' the property totally in the hands of the agent, and the agent may omit to mention some of the selling points which are not obvious to the applicant during a viewing.

However, some agents do an excellent job of showing property to prospective buyers, and are often better at it than the vendors themselves. If they are familiar with the geography of the building they will be able to conduct the tour with maximum ease and confidence. Familiarity of the agent with a property makes for a relaxed atmosphere during a viewing, although some would argue that if the agent has obviously visited the property many times before this implies the property has been on the market for some time.

TOP TIP
If inviting strangers into your home makes you uncomfortable, clarify with the agents before instructing them that they will accompany applicants during viewings .

As a compromise between either agent or vendor showing applicants around, some vendors opt for a joint effort with their agent, and this can work very well for several reasons:

- For vendors who are not confident of their selling abilities, an 'expert' is on hand.
- Activities which distract the vendor's attention (restraining children or answering the phone) do not interrupt the smooth running of a viewing.
- An experienced agent will know the difference between what the applicant needs to know and a confusing bombardment of information.
- The agent is known to the applicant as a familiar face which may put him at ease.
- If the applicant has a query about the property after the viewing he can talk it over with the agent who will understand what he is referring to.
- The vendor is able to supply 'invisible' information, like transport in the area or details of any improvements made to the property

, which will complete the picture (the agent cannot be expected to know everything about all the properties on his books).

- The applicant is more likely to give an honest opiion to the agent, whereas he may be reticent about being ungracious to the vendor.
- The presence of the vendor 'softens' the property into a home.
- The vendor (especially a lady or elderly person) may feel more at ease to have the agent on hand when inviting strangers into the property.

Sales techniques

For many people the idea of a salesman conjures up an image of a brash individual with slicked back hair and creased suit, peddling his wares with the subtlety of a rhino, and for them the prospect of having haemorrhoids removed with a rusty nail file is slightly more appealing than suffering five minutes with a timeshare salesman. But seriously now, in order to research this important chapter it was necessary to find out more about selling, and the first thing which becomes obvious is that we are all salesmen in one way or another. If you think you are not salesman material, then think again. The child who persuades his parents to buy a particular trendy item is indirectly selling that item. The mother who presents her child for acceptance into the best school is selling the child's abilities. At an interview we sell our skills, and every time we ask for a good deal or discount, we are selling our custom as the valuable commodity it is.

At almost every turn of life we are selling, so why is it so difficult for us to sell a property? The simple answer to that is that it isn't. But before we look at how to sell, we must first define 'selling' and determine what part a vendor can play in the success of a property sale. In order to do this we need first to make the distinction between selling and promoting, and whilst this chapter is designed to encourage vendors to take an active role in selling their property, and to realise their importance in this role, it would be quite wrong to dismiss the value of promotion or confuse the two.

• Promotion

Those vendors who do not use the services of an estate agent will need to promote the property themselves, which will entail advertising. In other words, they will need to attract an audience (or market) before they are in a position to make a sale. Those who do use an estate agent will not promote the property themselves. This is the agent's job, it is what he is being paid for, and is what he is best able to do. He will have a planned strategy to ensure adequate advertising, which will result in a valuable list of potential buyers as a customer base.

• Selling

Selling is described literally as disposing or transferring an item to a purchaser in exchange for payment. But it is the positive action (or not) of the vendor and his agent, ultimately resulting in the disposal or transfer, which establishes whether the sale is being conducted reactively or actively. The vendor must ask himself whether he is relying purely on the agent's promotion to achieve a sale (only becoming involved if and when a sale presents itself) or whether he is actively involved in achieving a sale by virtue of his dedication and sales input.

TOP TIP
By checking the agreement signed between vendor and agent you may find that vendors who additionally market their property independently, and who secure a sale by so doing, will still have to pay the agent a commission on the sale.

Having clarified the difference between selling and promoting, and employing an agent to take responsibility for the latter, the vendor needs to look at his role in the actual selling of the property and how effective it can be. Promotion does not work alone in securing a sale, and in order for it to be successful it needs to be followed up with active selling, which is where the vendor comes in. Whenever an applicant makes an appointment to view the property, the vendor is presented with a potential buyer, and given the opportunity of securing a sale. If he does not take advantage of this opportunity he cannot, in all fairness, blame the agent's role in promoting the property if the property remains unsold.

Unfortunately many vendors do not get involved in actually trying to sell their property, believing either that they are not blessed with selling skills (which we have already established they probably are) or fearing their ignorance of the mysterious 'housing market' will trip them up in some way. Some vendors even feel intimidated into leaving everything to the discretion of their selling agents, feeling there is very little they can do themselves to help achieve a sale. The reasoning for this comes in part from the seemingly endless complications which many vendors fear could present themselves should they become involved in a system which they assume they know nothing about, when in fact the whole process of agreeing a purchase and then transferring ownership from one party to another is actually not a complicated process. It doesn't always proceed from one stage to another very quickly, but there are few surprises along the way. If anything does cause an aborted sale, it is usually not the complexities of the system.

Many people believe that a salesman of property requires an in-depth knowledge of the housing market, experience of property law and tough negotiating skills (which they imagine estate agents have but they do not) when in fact all the vendor needs to take an important role in selling his own property is preparation, enthusiasm and effort.

Having faith in your product, knowing the market and having the correct approach are all important factors when selling anything, including property. However, the most important factors must be enthusiasm for the product and optimism for success. Who would buy anything from a salesman who clearly has no pride in his product and gives the impression that he does not expect the customer to buy it? Take a look at advertising to see how manufacturers proclaim their wares with enthusiastic advertising which says "Hey, this product is great." A certain lager manufacturer even has the confidence to proclaim its product as the best in the world – probably. In the same way, the vendor should proclaim the values of his property with enthusiasm and confidence, not plonk it on the market with little hope of a sale. If the vendor does not project the impression that the property is worth having, is it any wonder that the customer will pick up on this and have to agree?

DID YOU KNOW? *The customer must believe he is making the decision to buy, the salesman merely supplies the information to allow the customer to make the right decision.*

If your property is offered at a fair price, there is no reason why you should not feel confident to sell it as a desirable commodity. Have faith in your 'product' and your buyer will too. Above all, when viewing appointments are arranged, recognise the gift that has been granted you every time a potential buyer rings the door bell. You have a captive audience and, even better, one which is in 'buying mode'. The buyer has come to you specifically with the idea of buying; all you have to do is convince him that what you have is what he wants.

It would be impossible to do justice to all the theories of great salesmanship in one chapter, but shown below are several basics to give a background knowledge which could help vendors deal with customers more effectively.

Be prepared

To be prepared you must be like a good waiter and anticipate the customer's needs. When the agents makes an appointment for a potential buyer, ask about the type of people they are sending. If they are elderly, they may be interested in the community scene; if they have children then schools will be a priority. Get together as much information as possible on the aspects you think will interest a particular buyer, so that you can present your property in the right way. The more relevant information you can supply, by way of leaflets or verbally, the more 'plus points' your property has in it's favour when a prospective buyer comes to weigh up its benefits over other similar properties.

Try not to leave out anything which could create a query in the buyer's mind, and if there is something about the property which is obviously detrimental, try to think of some positive aspects about it. A buyer will not, for example, neglect to notice if the property is situated next to a petrol station, but the fact that the petrol station stocks a good range of groceries and that the people working there are very pleasant goes some way to lessen an obvious negative. It will be noticed anyway, so you might as well try to show it in a good light.

DID YOU KNOW?   *There is rarely any aspect of a property which cannot be displayed in a positive light with a little forethought and imagination – a tiny garden is a sun-trap with ease of maintenance.*

Needs and wants

When a customer decides to buy a product (in this case a property), he almost certainly has certain needs which must be met. These are things which are not negotiable, like the area, number of rooms and price range. Then there are certain criteria which can be classed as wants; things that would be preferable, like a downstairs cloakroom, side access or sea view. If your property doesn't satisfy the needs of the customer it is unlikely he will buy or even view, but assuming the needs have been met, you may be able to present some aspect of your property in such a way that it turns from a want into a need. Let us take for example a sea view. To the applicant, before viewing your property, it may be nice to have a view but not essential – it is therefore a want. However, having seen your property and succumbed to enthusiastic promotion of your sea view, any property he subsequently sees which does not have such a view will pale into insignificance. Thereby, you have turned a want into a need, which can only be met by your property.

Making buying easy

DID YOU KNOW? *When it comes to buying property, there are few pleasures in the 'shopping' process – people don't want to buy property, they just want to own it; as quickly and easily as possible.*

Ask any salesman the principles of good selling, and he will probably tell you that making buying easy is one of the main keys to success. So, following this lead, the vendor needs to make the prospect of buying his property as simple and uncomplicated as possible.

Firstly, be positive. If a potential buyer hesitates to make an offer over something rectifiable, perhaps because the property has no downstairs WC, the vendor could obtain a quote for plumbing, then try to reach a compromise on the purchase price to meet the installation costs. By doing so, the vendor is acting assertively and making things happen. Alternatively, he could give up on the sale immediately, declaring the viewing a waste of time and so gain nothing from the experience. Often all that is needed is imagination to see a solution to a negative reaction. There won't be a solution to everything and sometimes the vendor will have to give up on a particular sale, but if the vendor shows he is keen to sell by trying to resolve a problem without complicating matters, the buyer himself might be more likely to compromise. (See also Dealing with objections, below)

Secondly, try not to see problems where there are none, especially when dealing with the intricacies of timing. Considering the amount of paperwork crossing backwards and forwards between solicitors, the fickle nature of the buying public and the general snail's pace at which conveyancing seems to move, it is a wonder property transfers ever achieve their final goal. But usually they do, as long as the process does not become so complicated as to overwhelm the buyer into withdrawing. Unfortunately, vendors sometimes anticipate problems before they happen, usually because they have experienced aborted sales before. Rather than calmly dealing with each hiccup as it occurs, they adopt the 'what if' syndrome and look for problems, piling them up into an unconquerable mountain, then panic the buyer by putting too many obstacles in the way of his purchase. By doing this, the buyer is dissuaded from continuing with the purchase because he has been convinced by the vendor that the process is too complicated to ever reach its conclusion.

Lastly, be approachable. Sales have been lost by vendors who give the impression that they are not open to negotiations. Understandably the vendor is keen to indicate that he is not 'desperate' to sell, but in so doing he can imply to the buyer that there will be no compromise on price or anything else. The buyer then feels he will be battling all the way to completion against a vendor who may or may not conclude with the sale, and who could hold up proceedings because of a hostile attitude and unwillingness to keep the buyer happy.

The greeting and leaving ceremony

How potential buyers are received by vendors will influence their mood as they view the property, and nothing creates a negative feeling quite like an unwelcome reception. At the initial greeting, the vendor should be courteous without being too formal, friendly without being over familiar, and appear honest, reasonable and approachable. The vendor should introduce him or herself, and any other members of the household encountered on the tour, make eye contact with the potential buyers and show an interest in what they say. By conversing in a relaxed and confident manner, the vendor can often discover plenty of useful information during a viewing. By using open-ended questions to elicit more than 'yes' or 'no' answers, the vendor can establish what the buyers are looking for in a property, then supply the necessary information to match the requirements.

TOP TIP
A good salesman adapts his presentation to fit the market he is selling to.

All members of the household should strive to create a pleasant and relaxed atmosphere during a viewing, by showing they are happy to welcome potential buyers into their home, or at least act as if they are. Never show a room dominated by television watching, or arrange a viewing in the middle of a family meal. The buyer will feel like a spare part, and all your efforts to create an sociable atmosphere will have been wasted.

TOP TIP
Shaking hands at the end of a viewing, gives the impression that some sort of agreement has been reached.

Lastly, vendors should try to avoid crowding the hall when the viewer arrives. The person who has been nominated as tour guide should be the only person doing the initial greeting, thus limiting the number of people cluttering up the area. The last thing a viewer wants to be confronted with is exuberant dogs or curious children the second he walks through the door.

Showing off

When a buyer puts together all the information he has been given on the property, from agency details, additional printed information from the vendor, and verbal information given during a viewing, he should know every good aspect of the property there is to know. Whilst the vendor will avoid overloading a potential buyer with useless information during a viewing, he should nevertheless, in one way or another, inform the buyer of everything worth mentioning which promotes the property as a desirable product. So, if the loft is boarded, mention it; if the wiring has been updated, say so, and if your lights dim let them shine. If you decide to leave curtains and carpets, mention these, and why be shy about bringing attention to particularly good ones? Every positive aspect demonstrates value for money.

TOP TIP

Observe a professional car salesman in action to see how he draws attention to every 'extra' included in the price.

Deciding on the 'route'

Whilst the vendor will try not to omit showing anything important, he should take care to work out the best 'route' around the property during a viewing, pointing things out in an ordered fashion as he goes from room to room, so that the viewer does not leave with a complicated mental picture. Some people show the upstairs rooms first, some the downstairs and some the garden. Often the downstairs rooms have the best decoration, and since the kitchen and living room are usually the most important rooms to a buyer, some estate agents recommend the route starts with these rooms. Also, where the property has an extension or conservatory, the square footage downstairs will be greater. Salesmen who sell showhomes often start and end the route in the 'best' room, so that a potential buyer is given the opportunity to reaffirm the most attractive features of the property and leave with the good impression he started with.

> **TOP TIP**
> Generally speaking, the best features should be shown first, on the principle that first impressions last.

If there is room for expansion of improvement at the property, draw attention to it in a positive light. by trying to think of any realistic alterations and mentioning them. Maybe you have a large loft which could be converted to an extra bedroom, or an adjoining double garage, half of which would make an excellent playroom. This encourages a prospective buyer to use his imagination, and once he is doing this, he is picturing himself living there.

If you feel you have to explain each room, try to use a little imagination instead of simply saying "This is the kitchen." A room with a cooker and a sink speaks for itself as a kitchen, but you could introduce the room by saying "This is the room my husband/wife loves to spend time in; it's so sunny and has a lovely view over the garden.". This gives the room character whilst drawing in several positive points (the view and south facing aspect in this case).

Self presentation
Without wishing to make vendors self-conscious whilst conducting

viewings, it is worth mentioning that the vendor and anyone else at the property during a viewing will be noticed almost as much as the property itself. This is not a bad thing if the occupants make a good impression, but if they make a bad one the property could be remembered as 'the one with that chap who never stopped talking' or 'that house where a dreadful woman ...' If this is the case, the viewer will probably not remember much about the property, but the vendor will have made an unforgettable impression. So, as always, first impressions count. Dressing up is unnecessary, but bear in mind that you are a reflection not only of the property but also of the area, and your viewer will assume the neighbours are like you.

DID YOU KNOW?   *Retailers give their products a personality by using well known faces or voices of 'personalities' in their adverts, leading to an association between the product and the person. Similarly the vendor's personality reflects on the property.*

Timing your approach

A good salesman gains the confidence of his customers before he tries to sell them anything. A good salesman does not move in for the kill at entirely the wrong moment, in the wrong circumstances and with the wrong approach.

Consider for a moment the timeshare salesman who finds himself at the wedding of his brother to Lady Someoneorother. The bride's parents have done the happy couple proud with a reception at their country house. Champagne sparkles in the best crystal, canapés are served on polished silver platters by uniformed staff and all around an atmosphere of serene elegance prevails over the privileged guests. Now being a salesman of considerable diligence, such a gathering is to our timeshare chappie like a feast to the starving. Laid out before him is an audience which not only has no chance of escape, but also appears to be financially well endowed. Accordingly, no sooner has he been introduced to the in-laws, than he feels compelled to launch into his standard pitch on the dubious pleasure of sharing a half-built flat in Spain with several dozen other hapless people who, in a moment of insanity, also bought in.

Sadly, but not surprisingly, this none-too-subtle approach does not meet with any favourable responses, and our salesman goes home an unhappy man, having failed to come away with anything more than indigestion. The timing and approach was completely wrong, making the audience unreceptive.

And the moral of this tale when related to property selling? Don't try the hard sell on the doorstep, before your potential buyers have had time to consider everything they have seen and heard. Allow time for your subtle sales techniques to lay the foundations of a successful sale, then make contact through the agent the next day to see if there is any more information needed.

TOP TIP

Don't put people 'on the spot' by angling for a quick decision. If the vendor tries to hurry a firm decision from an applicant on whether or not he wants to buy the property, it is simpler for the applicant to say 'no' than 'yes' because he will not want to make a commitment at this early stage.

Try to relate to potential buyers and their needs. Our timeshare salesman would have fared better if he had first mingled unobtrusively, sizing up his audience to see which approach would best fit the type of gathering. Because he bungled in head-first, no-one felt an affinity towards him. Of course some salesmen survive because of the sheer number of approaches they make, not because of any keen selling skills, but unless you have people queuing up to view your property, this technique is not an option.

In all your sales techniques, assume the potential buyer will have a short attention span for verbal embellishment. The visual aspects of your property should not be clouded, so supplying extra written details of your own (floor plan, local information sheet etc.) will be more effective than bombarding buyers with verbal information as they tour the property, most of which they will forget.

Follow-ups

The vendor should insist that his agents contact each applicant after a viewing appointment to ascertain the applicant's impressions and answer any questions he might have. This is vitally important, since there could be some aspect of the property which has created a negative impression but which the agent can correct to save the sale. Even if the viewing went badly and the applicant was honest enough to say at the time that the property was not suitable, the vendor should still insist the agent makes contact to find out what in particular dissuaded an offer from being made. It may be something that can be altered or which the vendor can negotiate on, but if the reason is not known there is nothing anyone can do to reverse the decision. Also, if the vendor knows what disappointed one applicant, he may be able to rectify the problem before it has a similarly negative effect on the next applicant who views.

In some cases a vendor will market his property at a particular price, but make it known to the agent that he is willing to discuss offers below that price in certain circumstances. If the agent contacts all applicants after viewings, he can at that time use price negotiations to strike up a deal with an applicant who may not have been 100% committed to the purchase, but may in retrospect be tempted by a lower price. The agent may also be under instruction to use price negotiations to 'compensate' an applicant for whatever swayed him against making an offer. For example, if the absence of a garage is a stumbling block, the agent can alleviate this problem by saying that the purchase price could be negotiated to allow for the cost of construction (assuming planning permission can be obtained).

For post-viewing negotiations between applicant and agent to work, the vendor needs to be honest with the agent so that he, the agent, knows how far to go with negotiations. Being honest with one's agent is not something many vendors are prepared to contemplate, since a small number of estate agents have sullied the reputation of all the others by putting their own interests before that of their clients, which is not conducive to honesty. Some vendors think that by telling the agent their bottom line, i.e. the minimum selling price they can afford to let the property go for, they limit the ultimate price to that figure as a maximum because the agent will be glad to sell the property quickly as a bargain. Sadly it is not possible to refute this practice ever happens, but it is still preferable for a vendor to receive a low offer which he can choose to accept if he wishes, and may even be able to negotiate upwards, than not to receive any offers at all. (Vendors in Scotland should read Chapter 11, Procedures in Scotland, since they are bound to continue with the sale once an offer has been formally accepted.).

> **TOP TIP**
> Every viewing should be treated as if it was the first, with care, enthusiasm and good preparation.

Dealing with objections

For every rejection of the property, the vendor should discover the reason. Don't accept an 'off the cuff' objection (if you are given one) as a buyer is leaving. People generally find it very difficult to make disparaging remarks face to face, so you are unlikely to be told the real reason. "We really wanted something near the park," or "The garden is a bit big for us." are the sort of answers you might get. But ask yourself - why did they bother to view when they knew the location and the size of the garden from the property details? You are far more likely to get a truthful answer if the agents ask, but unfortunately they are not necessarily the best people to deal with the objection. For example, the objection may be that the property is 10 miles from the nearest town. This would probably seem, to the agent at least, an insurmountable objection and reason enough to assume that rejection is unavoidable. You, on the other hand, having already anticipated this objection, will switch the emphasis away from the distance and point out that the town is actually 'a very pleasant 15 minute drive away'.

A genuine objection often indicates a genuine interest – the buyer WANTS to find a solution. Let us take a situation where a couple are moving to a new area. They view a property which they like very much, but feel forced to decline to buy because the distance to the local school is too far for their son to walk to. The vendor, using his imagination and knowledge of facilities in the area, may be able to quash this objection by supplying what the couple really need, if they did but know it, which is information about a much better school accessible by a local bus which, by a happy coincidence, stops at the end of the road.

• Anticipating objections

If your property has been on the market for some time and are aware of the reason for this, you have the knowledge to anticipate future objections in advance of them being made. It may be something relatively simple, like the outside of the property requiring painting which is consistently putting buyers off. Don't allow potential buyers to see this as an impossible hurdle, raise the issue yourself with a carefully prepared counter-attack. In this situation the best recourse might be to obtain a quote for the work, then show that cost of the work is reflected in the asking price, or be prepared to negotiate.

• Damage limitation

Wherever possible, tie the buyer down to one specific objection. If he approves of everything else, you may be able to overcome or compensate for a single problem, and could still be in with a chance of securing a sale.

• Eliciting solutions

Sometimes people have their own answer to a problem. They know what the solution is for them, but fear it may come across as unreasonable, so they raise the objection but don't mention their idea of a solution. If someone raises a problem and you cannot think of a solution, ask them if they can think of any resolution which would make them happy. You might be agreeably surprised with a positive response.

• Clarifying objections

People say the strangest things, things which often bear no relation to what they actually mean. The buyer may say in a disparaging tone "It isn't a very big garden, is it?". If you say "Did you want a big garden?" they might say "No, not really, we wouldn't have time to look after it.". By insisting on clarification, the objection has been thrown back to establish whether there is a genuine problem, which in this case there is not.

Second viewings

If an applicant likes a particular property he may ask to visit it again, either to assure himself that the decision to buy is the right one before submitting an offer, or to refresh his memory after seeing lots of other properties. A second viewing is often misinterpreted by vendors as a sure indication that an offer is about to be made and the sale is in the bag, but this is not necessarily the case. With so many properties on the market, applicants often pay a second visit to several properties which they have short listed as 'possibles'. When a property is short listed for a second viewing, the vendor must make even more effort to impress because the competition, although thinned down, is more intense. Whilst each short-listed property shone amongst dozens of inappropriate properties, they are now being seen alongside others which are just as appropriate in terms of the basic requirements of size, location and price, and the applicant will now be looking for that little something extra to tip the balance in favour of one property over another.

DID YOU KNOW?   *Most people like a property less the second time they see it.*

An applicant will often be more relaxed during a second viewing. For a start he knows where he is going and how long it takes to get there, so will not arrive too early or late, and since he is now known to the vendor the door step greeting between the two parties is less formal. There is also an intimation that the applicant is definitely interested in the property, so a vendor who dislikes conducting viewings will perhaps be more inclined to treat the applicant as a serious buyer and not a time waster and so overcome any natural hostility over the intrusion into his privacy.

Given the element of familiarity between vendor and applicant during a second viewing, the vendor may be happy to allow the applicant a more informal tour of the property, at his own pace, unsupervised. Indeed some vendors feel they must allow this since to lead the applicant around a second time, when he is aware of the geography, would appear petty and unnecessary. However, vendors should not be intimidated into allowing unsupervised viewings unless they feel comfortable in so doing, and in any event it is wise to be aware of the risk of theft and take precautions over valuables and keys. However, there is a positive reason for allowing unsupervised viewings in that the applicant begins to feel 'at home' in the property and is better able to picture himself living there if he is not made to feel an intruder by the presence of the present owner. Of course this is precisely the response which can result in a sale.

During a second viewing, having already been impressed by the surface attractions of the property, the applicant may now look past these to affirm those things which are of particular relevance to him. Also, after impulsive enthusiasm, the applicant may be more concerned on his second visit with the condition of the property than just the aesthetics, and may even be disappointed to find his initial impression concerning size of rooms was deceptive one way or the other. Knowing this, the vendor needs to prepare the property with just as much care and attention for a second viewing as for the first - maybe even more.

For the vendor, viewings are the most important part of securing a sale. The agent will have done his bit in advertising the property and making the appointment, then it is all down to the vendor and the property. In the short space of time an applicant is viewing the property, the opportunity to make a sale presents itself – in fact this is the only opportunity for the vendor to make a sale. Once the buyer leaves the property there is no further way for the vendor to personally impress him into buying since any further contact will almost certainly be through the selling agent. If the vendor conducts a viewing badly, either with poor sales techniques or inadequate presentation, this golden opportunity will have been wasted.

In summary:

- Appreciate the importance of ALL viewings; treating each one with as much care as the last.
- Work with the selling agent to make sure that any viewings which can possibly be arranged, are arranged.
- Brush up on your sales techniques. Recognise that the vendor of a property can do a great deal to bring about a sale; possibly more than the selling agents.
- Insist that the selling agents follow up every viewing with a telephone call to the applicant.
- Treat second viewings with as much care and attention as initial viewings.

SHOW HOMES -
LEARNING FROM THE EXPERTS

The 'second hand' property market (you and I), has to compete with builders of new homes for buyers, just as second hand car salesmen compete with smart dealerships and second hand furniture shops compete with major retailers. But there is a glaring difference with selling second hand property, in that while the property is usually promoted through a retail outlet (an estate agency) it is actually 'sold' by the vendors themselves during face-to-face viewings. Estate agencies do not buy property from the general public and then sell it, whereas second hand car dealers and furniture shops do. If estate agencies had to invest in 'stock', and then dispose of it first hand, they would become retailers and need to employ professional salesmen to sell their product. As it is, second hand property is sold by amateurs, i.e. the vendors. The only true property retailers are new home builders, from whom vendors can learn a great deal by observing their approach to applicants and learning some of the tricks of the trade.

One of the first challenges for the salesmen and women who's job it is to sell new homes 'on site', is that they have only a limited number of home types available for sale on each particular site. The buildings may be a mixture of styles, but no one site will have something for everyone, so the salesman has to make the product fit the market. There might not be any flats for example, so the salesman must try to encourage those buyers looking for a flat to consider buying a house instead, or else rule out a section of potential buyers. On most sites the small- to mid-sized properties sell first, so the salesman is often faced with the problem of selling a surplus of large homes which must achieve a higher selling price, making them particularly difficult to dispose of.

The salesman's skills are further challenged because, unlike an estate agency, he does not have a range of locations to offer potential buyers, but must sell the site itself. This can seem almost impossible in the early stages of building work, when sites are a mess of rubble and mud, but such is the power of a well presented show home that even in the depths of a housing recession buyers will commit themselves to purchasing a home which is not even built.

We, as individuals trying to sell our homes, are similarly restricted in that we are not able to offer a choice of building or location. A potential buyer who receives details of our home will either like the style or not; it will either suit their requirements or it won't. A three bedroom town house simply will not sell to someone who needs several acres of land, nor will it sell to a student who wants a studio flat. You cannot please all of the people all of the time, but while the designers of show–homes recognise this, they do their best to attract the widest possible market by capitalising on mass appeal. They recognise the things which most people like, or at least do not object strongly to. A pale colour scheme for example, appeals to most people and offends very few, whereas bright red walls and black furniture will only appeal to a minority and so is not used in show–homes.

DID YOU KNOW?   *New home builders aim to appeal to the market most prevalent in the site area, by building homes similar to existing properties.*

House builders spend a great deal of time and money preparing show homes to tempt purchasers to buy their properties, and much can be learnt from them. Firstly, the salesman or woman who greets prospective buyers on site will have received training in sales techniques and will know how to deal with enquiries. He or she will have all the relevant information about the properties to hand, and will be able to show prospective buyers a carefully presented product. In short, the sales staff have all the ingredients necessary to achieve successful sales - professional techniques, good promotional material and a saleable product. By observing how show-homes are presented and the sales techniques used by trained property salesmen, vendors are able to pick up skills which may help to sell their own property.

Professional techniques

A good new home salesman does not make assumptions about applicants. He will not assume, for example, that a poorly dressed applicant will only be interested in property of a size or price befitting his appearance, neither will he ever dismiss an applicant out of hand as a 'time waster'. Whilst his gut feelings are finely tuned to enable him to sniff out genuine buyers at twenty paces, usually by the type of questions they ask, the salesman will nevertheless treat every applicant as a possible buyer, just in case. A good salesman will also 'read' the mood and needs of each applicant, knowing when to talk and when to stay silent, so that he can promote those things which could be overlooked without dominating proceedings with excessive or irrelevant chatter.

Often the salesman or woman gives the applicant the choice of whether they would like to be accompanied on their tour of the showhome, or whether they would like to look round on their own. Some applicants prefer to look first then ask questions, and a good salesman will speak to applicants after they have viewed to provide information and promotional material. To enable the salesman to 'catch' the applicant after he has viewed the show-home and before leaving the site, many show-homes are accessed through the sales office. If the show-home is small and more than one applicant comes to view it at the same time, the salesman will often encourage each applicant to look around separately so that the show-home does not appear crowded. This may entail the salesman entertaining one of the applicants until the other has finished looking around, but as an affable host, the good salesman will supply the waiting applicant with plenty of information and literature to whet his appetite before he views the show-home. If the show-home is large enough not to be crowded by more than one applicant, the salesman may encourage multiple viewings which gives the agreeable impression that the property is attracting plenty of interested buyers and is in demand.

A good site salesman will always make every effort to take the name, address and telephone number of all applicants who call at the site and will contact them, usually by telephone the following day, to bring the site back to their attention and to answer any queries. If an applicant is unhappy about some aspect of the property, the salesman is then in a position to negotiate a solution to the problem and in this way prompt, or salvage, a sale which might otherwise have been missed.

Finally, a good salesman or woman will make sure the show-home always looks its best, checking it between viewings and at the start of each day to make sure nothing is out of place.

DID YOU KNOW?   *You do not sell an object, you sell the benefits of that object. People do not buy a television as an object of decoration, they buy it for its entertainment value. Similarly we do not buy a property because of the shelter it offers, but rather for emotional benefits of cosmetic pleasure, status or convenience.*

Promotional material

Another thing which becomes apparent when viewing a show-home is the amount of literature you come away with. The sales negotiator will be very keen to provide plenty of colourful information about the homes because the more literature a prospective buyer reads, the more time he spends considering the property.

Why not take a tip from the professionals and create an

information pack about your property? Estate agents prepare factual property details, but there is no reason why vendors should not prepare their own extra literature for viewers to take away with them after a viewing. The information must be truthful and not misleading, so it is a good idea to ask your agent to read through the contents to make sure it is suitable and proper. An enthusiastic collection of information certainly sets one property apart from all the rest and helps to prolong the applicants interest after the viewing is over. The following could be included:

- Floor plan (if not to scale, make sure you say so).
- Extra colour photographs.
- Area information (you may be able to get this from the local Tourist Board).
- Transport available/commuting times/schools.
- Details of any planning permission obtained, (outline or detailed).
- Your own written description of each room and the gardens etc.

House builders almost always produce stylish promotional material which goes way beyond the scope of that which estate agents typically provide. The site office will usually have wall displays including an artist's impression of each style of home, the relevant floor plans and a plan of the site itself showing which homes are still available and which have been sold, and their relation to each other. The attractively designed material for applicants to take away with them is not limited to a photograph of the property and a rundown on the size of each room, and often includes much additional information about the area. They are aware that they must not only sell the bricks and mortar, but also the site itself and the community which will be living there. For this reason, you will notice that the artist's impression often includes attractive people with charming children standing outside the property looking very happy and content in their surroundings. The promotional material given to applicants may also include information about the type of heating, the construction and energy efficiency (double glazing etc.). All this gives potential buyers the impression that the builders are proud of the buildings and are not afraid to promote everything about them in a positive way.

Saleable product

The most important weapon the new homes salesman has at his disposal is the show–home itself. This is in effect a promotional sample of the other buildings for sale on the site; a prototype if you like, and is used as an advertisement on how your home could look, in much the same way as a model shows how the customer buying a particular shampoo could look after using that product. The customer's hair may not be the same colour or style as the model's so it probably won't work, and the prospective buyer's furniture and effects won't be the same colour or style as those in the show home, but we can all dream, and it is the applicants' dreams and aspirations of how they want their new home to look which is capitalised on so effectively by a good show home.

One of the first things noticeable on visiting a show home is the amount of light. Even in the middle of the day, all the rooms invariably have lights on, and no expense has been spared outside in lighting paths, garages, doorsteps etc. The effect of this is psychological, a bit of emotional manipulation. People respond favourably to light – it gives them a sense of well-being in the same way that sunlight brings a smile, and if a prospective buyer feels good in a property he is more likely buy it.

The second thing to notice is the careful positioning of 'personal effects' and what those personal effects are. Books fill bookcases and glossy magazines are placed neatly on coffee tables, but you won't

127

find yesterday's crumpled newspaper lying on the floor. The kitchen invariably has fake fruit in a bowl and the breakfast bar will be cosily set with colour co-ordinated crockery, but half empty milk cartons and the horrors of a sink full of washing up are banished.

When people enter a show–home, they usually feel comfortable and relaxed. And so they should, since the decoration will have been picked for mass appeal and follows the fashion of the day. More importantly, visitors to a show–home will probably feel they could quite happily live there. Of course in reality, most of us couldn't keep up with such neat perfection for long, and neither would we want to, but we think we would at the time of viewing. Having good marketing material to hand and the ability to actively sell go some way towards explaining the successful selling of new homes, but the biggest impact on the applicant (in his opinion at least) is the quality of the product. For this reason, builders prepare show–homes as a life sized product display.

DID YOU KNOW?   *To give an impression of space, some builders do not hang the interior doors in their show-homes.*

One of the main gripes about new homes is often that they are too small, but because the cost of land is so high, builders have to squeeze as many properties as they can onto a site to make it a financially viable project, and this can lead to the properties themselves having cramped internal accommodation. This is where the interior designers of show–homes use their skill in careful planning and thoughtful preparation to make the best use of the available space, without making the rooms feel small or crowded. So how do they do it?

- Firstly, they do not include any items which are neither necessary nor attractive as a display, so there are unlikely to be linen baskets and medicine cabinets in the bathroom or dustbins in the kitchen. In the study you may find an attractive bookcase, but a filing cabinet and the clutter of stationery will not be included. In the living room you will not find a fire guard, unless it is decorative and televisions, hi-fi units and speakers are rarely evident.

- Items of furniture used in a show–home are usually in a pale colour scheme, will have been carefully arranged and are often of smaller than average size to make the room look large in comparison.
- Beds are always made up and any soft furnishings, like curtains and carefully arranged cushions, are colour co-ordinated.
- Curtains are never closed or untidily arranged, but are usually draped or tied back to exaggerate the size of the windows
- Rugs are rarely used because they clutter the room, and the carpets are often plain and pale to emphasises an expanse of clear floor area.
- Walls are usually decorated in pale colours which reflect light, increase the feeling of space, and will not offend anyone. The style of decoration is often aimed to appeal to female applicants and will steer away from anything too austere or masculine.
- Doors are left open so as not to restrict the space or block light.
- Designers of show homes try to make the rooms appear 'lived in' by including pictures on the walls, flowers, fluffy towels in the bathroom and the tables are almost always set for a meal, both in the dining room and kitchen.
- The rooms are well illuminated and warm, and any decorative fires are lit even in the summer months.
- Since the smell of a property is one of the first thing to hit a person on entering, many show–homes have bowls of potpourri in each room to make sure the smell is pleasant.
- When the salesman escorts an applicant around a show–home, he will usually invite the applicant to enter each room first, so that he

stays out of the line of vision and does not himself crowd the limited space.

DID YOU KNOW?   *The kitchen and living room are considered by many house builders to be the rooms which most influence a sale.*

Show-homes are not designed as a reflection of normal daily life, any more than catwalk models are an example of normal everyday people; they are more of an 'ideal' or aspiration, and are presented to give the best possible impression of comfort and aesthetic appeal. For most of us our homes do not, and should not, look like a show–home. They are used and enjoyed by real people and as such portray an intimacy and style which show–homes lack. However, for the purposes of selling a home, it is worthwhile for vendors to observe the way show–homes are presented and learn from the salesmen who use them as a sales tool.

In summary:
- If possible, visit some show–homes to observe the sales techniques of the salesmen.
- Prepare your own 'promotion pack' of additional material relating to the property and the area.
- Observe the way show–homes are presented, and apply any suitable techniques to your own property.

REVIEWING THE SITUATION

Identifying the problem

There comes a time, if all efforts to secure a sale so far have failed, when the vendor needs to sit down and review the situation. It may be that the housing market is particularly slow at the time, or that the property is of a type which only appeals to a small section of the buying public, for example properties which are:

- very expensive, very large or very small
- particularly unusual, like converted chapels
- listed buildings with strict restrictions
- not mortgageable, maybe because of structural damage
- positioned badly; possibly on a very busy road or next to a railway

These properties could take considerably longer to sell than usual, in which case the vendor may need to accept this and, so long as he is satisfied that promotion of the property is adequate, there may be little more he can do to achieve a sale other than make sure the property is presented to suit the price and that viewings are conducted well

However, if the property is comparable with others which are selling and market conditions are fair, there must be a reason why the property has not sold and this needs to be identified and dealt with accordingly if the position is to be rectified.

Firstly, the vendor needs to ascertain whether the problem lies with the promotion or the property itself, and one way to do this is to look at the viewing pattern. If there have been very few viewings from which to secure a sale, this could be for two reasons. Either:

- the property is not being brought to the attention of the right applicants, or
- applicants are receiving details, but something is dissuading them from viewing.

If on the other hand there are a satisfactory number of viewings but no offers are resulting, this could be because either:

- some negative aspect of the property, apparent during a viewing, is dissuading applicants from making an offer, or
- the property is simply not standing up against competition from comparable properties.

1. Lack of viewings

In some cases a lack of viewing appointments can point to inadequate promotion by the estate agent, although this is not always the case and it could just be that the agent is very thorough when 'matching' applicants to property. If there are no viewings at all, maybe the agents are being a bit too thorough in their matching, or perhaps their type of promotion is not reaching the right applicants for that particular property, in which case a change of agents might be worth considering.

• Changing the agent

If the property is not promoted well the chances of a sale are dramatically decreased. Since agency promotion is usually the only way potential buyers get to hear of a property's availability, poor promotion means perilously few customers to sell to. Naturally then, from time to time it is worth re-evaluating the services a vendor is receiving from the selling agent, and as a measure of the agency's continuing suitability vendors should ask themselves the following:

- Is the agency in regular contact, or do the staff seem to have lost interest?
- Is the property still advertised regularly?
- Are the property details still prominently displayed in the office?
- Is the agency keen to offer further promotions or do they appear to have they exhausted their avenues of sales options?

If your answers to the above are negative, it is time for a chat with the manager before deciding whether or not to change agents. Call into the office or telephone, explain you are disappointed with the response so far and ask what the next step will be to further promote the property. This puts the ball firmly into the agent's court and demands active suggestions. Alternatively, be up-front and say you will give the agents another fortnight or so to effect a sale, after which time the property will be withdraw from their register. They will not want to see a client, or more importantly a commission, sailing off into the sunset, the very thought of which may spur them into action and renew flagging interest.

If this doesn't work you may decide to change agents, in which case you should be just as careful with your second choice as you were with your first. Looking on the bright side though, at least you have already done your homework on the agents in the area, so the selection process should be easier the second time around.

TOP TIP

If you are buying your next property in the same area you are selling in, you will have first hand experience of how the local agents treat potential buyers. If, as a result of your own property search, you come across an agency which shines out from the rest, they will be the obvious choice as your new selling agents.

When considering changing agents, be aware of the following if you have entered into a sole agency Agreement with your original agents.

a) If you achieve a sale through a second agent but have not either terminated your Agreement with the original agency or else altered the Agreement from sole to multiple agency, you could be liable to pay commission to both the original agent (at their multiple agency rate) and the one who introduced the purchaser.

b) If, having changed agents, a sale is secured by way of a past introduction by the original agents, you could be liable to pay commission to the second agent under his current Agreement and to the original agents since the introduction came through them.

• Increasing circulation

Sometimes vendors use a selling agent who is competent and reliable, and makes every effort to achieve a sale, but still fails to find a buyer because his promotion is not reaching enough applicants. This can happen in towns or cities which have a large population and many agents, each of whom covers their own small area. In this situation, potential buyers only become aware of those properties being promoted through the particular agents they approach for written details. Since they may not approach every agent in each area, they will not hear of property being sold by the agencies which are not approached. The circulation of an agency operating through only one office will not be as extensive as a larger company with several offices covering surrounding towns, who will tend to promote all the properties on their books through all their offices and so net a wider catch of potential buyers.

  If the vendor feels the lack of viewings is a result of poor circulation, he may wish to continue using the existing agency because their services are not cause for complaint, but increase circulation by instructing another agency as well, under a multiple agency arrangement. When deciding to change from sole to multiple agency the first step should be to contact the existing agent and tell them your decision, explaining that you want to attract a wider audience by increasing agency representation. Make it plain that you are impressed with their excellent service so far and would like it to continue, so that you keep them interested enough to persevere on your behalf and avoid putting anyone's nose out of joint. Under the terms of your existing agency Agreement you will probably be required to give notice of the intention to change from a sole to multiple agency arrangement, which gives the agent an opportunity to make every effort to find a buyer quickly, before he is put in competition with another agent.

It is easy to see the advantage of increasing circulation, but the disadvantage of over-exposure should not be ignored, and if a property is pushed by several agents with a regularity verging on desperation, the impression to potential buyers could be that there is something wrong with it.

• Going it alone

For some people, selling without an agent is a first choice, whilst to others going it alone comes about because they have become dissatisfied with the results of their selling agents and feel they could do a better job of promoting the property themselves. And maybe they can. However, although estate agents are unpopular and often employed grudgingly, their services usually do work, eventually. It is tempting to imagine that the high commission charged by agents is easy money, without realising the huge amount of wastage involved in the whole system of estate agency. This wastage is something that anyone contemplating selling their property privately should understand.

If, let us say, an agent is invited to value 100 properties a month, maybe only around 40 vendors will actually instruct him to sell. The others will either choose a different agent or change their mind about selling altogether for one reason or another. Of those 40 who become clients, some will be time-wasters 'testing the market', some will cancel the instruction before the agent finds a buyer, and still others will fall by the wayside as a result of changed circumstance. So, of the 40 original instructions, maybe 10 will result in a successful sale. If this still sounds like easy money, consider the man hours involved in the initial 100 valuations, the cost of producing written details for the 40 instructions and circulating these to perhaps hundreds of applicants, not to mention the overheads of staff, office premises and administration. Add to this the high costs of advertising and a telephone bill to bring tears to your eyes, and you have some idea of the financial wastage involved.

The reason for pointing this out to those who decide to go it alone, is that they should be prepared for the wasted costs they may incur. Estate agency commissions seem high when considering the amount of financial outlay dedicated to an individual client but, as shown above, expenses incurred from the 100 initial valuations must be borne by the 10 eventual paying customers. If you go it alone, be prepared to encounter time wasters, ineffective advertising and personal intrusion. At least when using an agency you know the property will probably sell eventually, and if not, or you decide not to sell for some reason, the promotion will have cost you nothing because most agents work on a 'no sale no fee' basis, whereas the vendor who handles his own sale could incur high personal costs whilst still failing to secure a sale.

• Approaching a different market

In the case of properties which have a limited market, a local agency may not have the right resources. Very large properties require different promotion to the average home, and an unusual property may need more widespread media promotion than that offered by local newspapers, which is for many agents the only avenue of media representation to which they subscribe.

Alternatively the vendor may re-evaluate the property's potential market and aim it at a different section of buyers. A large residential property, for example, could be attractive to the commercial market if promoted with potential to, say, convert into several flats (assuming any necessary planning consents are obtained). A commercial property like a village post office, might reach a wider audience if promoted as a residential house with the option of ceasing its current trade, rather than a commercial property with coincidentally has living accommodation. It may presently be promoted for it's commercial appeal with the residential accommodation as secondary, when perhaps it would cast a wider net of potential buyers if it's dual use was reversed in importance and promoted firstly as a house, with the post office as secondary.

Image is also important. There are agents who deal specifically with the higher end of the property sector who have the image to match. This is no more elitist than the clothing industry splitting itself into couture and 'high street' fashion, and the right type of agency is essential, especially for properties which fall into a category which is outside the scope of the average estate agency's promotional expertise.

• Dropping the price

If, on reflecting why the property is not attracting viewings, you suspect that an over-optimistic valuation could be the cause, speak to your agents and ask for their honest opinion – if they say price is not the problem, then it probably isn't. However, if they can demonstrate that the property is over priced in comparison with other comparable properties they are currently marketing, then you might need to think about dropping the price. How much you reduce by will depend on:

- What you can afford.
- How much you can pass on. If you accept less for this property, you might be able to pass the loss on by reducing your offer for your next property.
- Comparable prices.
- The impact level. If the current price is £104k, reducing to £99,950 will make more of an impact than reducing to £100,000 simply because there are fewer digits involved.

TOP TIP

If you drop the price of your property, make sure you get further promotion from the estate agency like an additional mail-shot to registered clients and extra advertising.

There are two schools of thought on advertising a price reduction. One is that a reduced price puts buyers off because they feel there must be something wrong with the property, while the other is that there is little point in lowering the price if you do not advertise the fact. Personally, I adhere to the latter. While a new price will automatically influence future buyers, if the reduction is not promoted it will be overlooked by those people who have already received details of the property but have dismissed it on grounds of price. Estate agents generally circulate property details within specific price ranges, so a reduction places the property within the reach of those for whom it was previously too expensive, introducing a whole new group of customers.

If after careful thought you are still uncertain whether a price reduction is the answer, you could consider a reduction for a limited period for, say, offers received before Christmas, which allows the market to be tested to see if a reduction has any effect. It would be foolish to reduce the price only to discover that this is not the reason for not attracting viewings.

• Open house

Definitely not for the feint hearted, an open house viewing day may be considered in cases where the agents receive 'interest' in a particular property (by which they mean the written details are regularly requested by applicants), but this interest does not result in viewings. Not all agents approve of this method of prompting viewings, and it is only really feasible if plenty of applicants have shown an interest in the property but have so far not viewed, and usually only if there is more than one prospective buyer in the property at any one time, to excite a sale from an impression of demand. Agents have differing views on the success of open house days, but most agree that issuing an invitation for all and sundry to drop in on an appointed day, without appointment, is a pretty desperate course of action. Apart from the practicalities of people wandering round your home with little or no supervision, consider also the curiosity value which will be irresistible to time-wasters.

Having said that, an open house does sometimes result in a sale, and it is just possible that someone may have received details and dismissed the property as unsuitable but, happening by chance to pass on the open day, feels tempted to call in and is duly impressed. Or perhaps someone calls in out of curiosity and is so taken with the property that they make an offer there an then. Unlikely, but possible.

Some people use open days instead of estate agents and advertise themselves. Others decide on an open day with the co-operation of their agent, in which case the vendor could ask the agent to either assist at the property on the day, or agree to a reduction in the fee if a sale results, bearing in mind the vendor did most of the work to ultimately achieve a sale.

The agents will deal with advertising, but the vendor should make sure he is happy with the extent of it, since in return for the considerable effort on his part, there must be adequate publicity, including a mail shot to registered applicants, if an open day stands any chance of success.

TOP TIP

During an open day it can promote interest to give the impression to those who have just arrived that they are in competition with hoards of other applicants who just left. Human nature being what it is, we always want what is popular. Don't over do it though - you don't want anyone to be dissuaded from making an offer because they think the competition is too high.

- Children and pets might be best excluded from the scene if possible.
- Put away valuables, especially those which are pocket sized.
- Call in the help of friends or family to position themselves around the property, both for security and to answer any questions.
- Prepare sandwiches or snacks in advance. These can be consumed by you and your helpers in a quiet moment, and do not necessitate messing up the kitchen or filling the property with food smells.
- If you are using an agent, obtain a pile of their written details (as well as your own floor plan etc.) which can be handed out on arrival.

2.Viewings, but no offers

A property which is attracting viewings but not offers has an advantage over one which is not attracting viewings, in that it is possible to ascertain, from the applicants who view, what it is about the property which is preventing a sale. There may be a whole range of different reasons, or one aspect of the property which is persistently stopping applicants from making an offer, or it could simply be that the property is failing to rise above competition from comparable properties. Whatever the reason(s) the vendor and his agent can work together to find out what is hindering the sale and either solve the problem or compensate for it.

• Improving presentation

The first step for the vendor is to be honest with himself. If the agents are promoting the property sufficiently to attract viewings but the property is being not being presented well and the vendor is making little effort to encourage a sale, then he has no-one to blame but himself. A good agent will be happy to come to a property and give advice on what he thinks could improve the chances of a sale (it is after all in his interest to do so), and if the vendor feels he is not the best person to conduct the viewings then maybe the solution is to ask the agent to conduct them instead. If, however, there seems no obvious reason why viewings are not progressing to offers, and the vendor is not willing to wait for an eventual sale, he may want to stimulate an offer.

• Price negotiations

When an applicant views several similar properties, all of which meet his basic requirements, then price will ultimately decide which one he offers to buy and those which he dismisses. That is not to say that one property cannot command, and achieve, a higher price than another because it is superior in some way, but most potential buyers are, in the final analysis, greatly influenced by price. When applicants arrange a viewing based on the written details, they already know, and presumably accept as reasonable, the price of the property before they view it. If price then becomes an issue, it must follow that, on closer inspection during the viewing, the property is not coming up to the applicants' expectations. Most applicants will make an offer which they feel is suitable, even if it is much lower than the asking price, if they like the property sufficiently and feel there is a possibility the offer will be accepted. However if applicants are not making offers at all, even low ones, then the selling price sought could be beyond the realms of possibility.

Some applicants need to be stimulated into making an offer by inference that the vendor may be willing to reduce the price. The vendor who wishes to stimulate offers in this way will need to discuss with his agent the reduction in price he is willing to consider, so that the agent can mention this after any future viewings and also contact applicants who have already viewed to see if they can be tempted to make an offer based on this new information. (See also Chapter 9, Negotiating the price.)

Part exchange

For vendors who cannot afford to wait indefinitely for a sale, a part exchange deal with a builder of new homes may be the quickest way of disposing of the property, assuming they are going to buy another, usually more expensive, property. Many builders of new homes offer part exchange deals to stimulate their sales by making their property accessible to potential buyers who are having difficulty selling their existing home. The system begins with the builder obtaining a valuation on the property to be part-exchanged and then submitting an offer. If this offer is acceptable the builder will, on conclusion of the transaction, receive the vendor's property (and usually a balance of cash to make up his asking price), in exchange for one of his new properties. In so doing the builder improves his cash-flow in the short term and eventually sells the surplus part-exchanged property, whilst his buyer moves into his new home with the minimum of hassle and delay.

A different type of part–exchange arrangement worked well for a couple who owned an expensive flat in an exclusive location and had difficulty finding a buyer when they came to sell it. Eventually they were presented with an applicant who was keen to buy but who had not sold his own bungalow and had no real prospect of doing so quickly. Given that the applicant had to sell his property before being in a position to buy the flat, the couple decided to circumvent the

142

stalemate by 'swapping' their flat for the applicant's small bungalow in the country (which is where they wanted to be anyway) plus an extra sum of cash. A very satisfactory conclusion all round.

DID YOU KNOW?   *Part exchange deals with new home builders are invariably only available for those who are considering a step up the housing ladder.*

In summary:
- Identify why the property is not attracting viewings, or else why the viewings are not resulting in offers.
- Consider what options are open to either widen circulation and so increase the number of viewings, or prompt offers from those applicants who are viewing.

SELLING AT AUCTION

Auction sales only account for a small percentage of overall property sales. Many vendors who consider selling at auction only do so as a last resort when their home has not attracted a buyer on the open market. Some vendors would like to use the auction system but find that their property is not suitable, and those who do have the right type of property often do not consider auctions because they have misconceptions about the mechanics of the system. From the buyer's perspective, part of the reason why auction rooms are not filled to capacity every week with eager bidders is that many people wrongly assume that they are unable to buy through auctions, or are apprehensive about the process, believing it to be more difficult than buying by the common method of private treaty.

Auctions are not a fail-safe way of selling, any more than any other way. There are no guarantees and to some extent the success of the auction relies simply on who attends the auction on the day, but there are advantages to selling at auction in that it is quick and, perhaps more importantly, once a buyer is found the chances of an aborted sale are negligible. However, auctions are not infallible, and if the auction is unsuccessful the chances of a subsequent sale on the open market are affected. In addition, the type of property which sells successfully will not encompass many homes, and the type of person who buys at auction is limited to a relatively small section of the buying public.

This chapter attempts to lay some of the popular misconceptions to rest and explain the auction system simply. Some selling agents handle auction sales slightly differently from others, so anyone wanting to find out more should speak with their local agents who will be able to advise on a particular property's chances of success at auction, and give specific information about auctions in the area.

Who buys at auction?

One of the first things a vendor must realise about an auction is that it needs to attract competition, otherwise the items up for sale, whether property or fine art, will not reach a good price. The system of an auction relies on more than one buyer being interested in each property and so bidding against each other to raise the price with each bid. Without this competition between buyers the auction system falters at the first hurdle and properties are at best sold cheaply; at worst not at all. So, if the auction and the properties which are to be disposed of are not marketed well enough or widely enough to attract a large audience, the auction will inevitably fail. The selling agents must therefore ensure that a wide audience is reached and that the potential buyers who attend are not only plentiful in number but are also the right type of buyers for the properties on offer. Adequate promotion of an auction has never been more essential than it is now, since in a housing market which has seen a decline in property sales generally, auctions do not attract the sheer number or diversity of buyers they used to.

Nowadays those buying at auction are most likely to be owner occupiers; people who are buying a single property as a home and not looking to make a profit. They may be looking to acquire a property which, were it not sold at auction in a poor state of repair, they might not ordinarily be able to afford, but they will not be looking to speculate on the property market. This is a far cry from the 1980's when the property market was volatile and fast moving. In those days, builders large and small were seen at auctions buying property which was then renovated and re-sold for a healthy profit, and enthusiastic DIY homeowners frequently looked to auctions for suitable investment properties to 'do up' then re-sell. Since the decline in the property market, builders and speculators are not nearly so prevalent at auctions. Whilst they may still be able to acquire the same type of properties, they are not able to re-sell quickly, and the time a renovated property remains unsold eats away at any profit they might have been able to achieve.

Suitable properties for auction

Not all properties are suitable for selling at auction, so vendors who make enquiries about this form of selling should be prepared to accept that some selling agents may refuse to auction a property if they do not feel it is suitable. The reason selling agents are selective in the properties they are prepared to auction, and why they will dismiss those which do not stand a good chance of success, is because it reflects badly on their reputation if they take a property to auction which does not reach its reserve. In addition, the amount of time and money an agent spends on promoting a property for auction is considerably more than for open market sales, so they must balance their resources against the chances of achieving a sale. Some agents charge a 'mortgage offering fee', but those who work on a strictly 'no sale no fee' basis will have wasted a lot of time and advertising revenue if the property does not sell. They will also lose face in the eyes of the vendor whose property does not reach its reserve, and any future vendors who make enquiries about their history of auction success will not be impressed by failures. Under normal circumstances agents are keen to have as many properties on their books as possible, so it is unusual for them to decline an instruction. However, while it is not in the agent's best interest to refuse to auction a property if there is a chance it will sell, vendors should appreciate that if an agent declines to auction a property because he feels it will not sell, he is probably right.

In theory almost any type of property can be sold at auction, but only at the right price. To achieve a reasonable sale price, one which reflects the true value, requires the right type of property. Given that so many buyers at auction are owner occupiers, the broad ingredients for the type of property which successfully sells at auction are:

146

- Worth less than £100,000.
- Constructed with individuality and charm.
- In need of modernisation and/or improvement.
- Situated in an area which is attractive - not necessarily an up- market area, but not underprivileged.

TOP TIP

If selling an unoccupied property which needs renovating (maybe a deceased estate) selling agents usually recommend that it is cleared of furniture and effects before viewings are arranged, and that the garden is cleared to make sure access is not hindered.

Properties which attract a good competitive audience are often situated in rural locations, typically a character cottage, although these tend not to be priced at the upper end of the property market. The golden rule governing the price of most auction properties is the cheaper the better, and a successful auction property will usually have a subjective value, i.e. its price will not be comparable with a similar property near by. In short, a property most likely to sell at auction will be a pretty country house, priced within the reach of a lot of buyers, and one which encourages an emotional response influenced more by the buyer's heart than his head.

The above criteria is not the only type of property which is sold at auction, but rather the most successful for private vendors. Building societies and banks use auctions to dispose of properties which they have repossessed and these properties are just as likely to be modern estate semis as pretty rural cottages. However, the building societies and banks are concerned primarily with disposing of the properties quickly, and will often settle for a price which is below the current market value. If a private vendor decides to sell a repossession type property at auction, he is likely to find himself in competition with banks and building societies for a buyer, which may necessitate matching or improving on the amount of 'discount' they will be prepared to accept.

Pricing for auctions

Selling agents will visit the property to assess its value in the same way they would for an open market sale, and then give their opinion on the price they think the property will achieve at auction and also the price they suggest would be most suitable for marketing purposes, i.e. the guide price.

• Guide Price

This is the price which the agent displays on the property details and in advertisements, and is likely to be lower than the final selling price. Vendors should not be discouraged if a low guide price is suggested by the agent (which it invariably is), since the guide price is designed primarily to encourage people to look, and does not necessarily have any reflection on the final selling price or the suggested reserve price.

• Reserve Price

This is the lowest price the vendor is willing to sell for, and the auctioneer will not accept a bid which is lower than this amount. If no-one bids at or above the reserve price, the property will remain unsold so it is important to be realistic when setting this level if you are keen to sell quickly. The reserve price will not necessarily be the level at which the auctioneer starts the bidding, since he will want to attract plenty of lively bids from the start. The level of the reserve price is usually discussed by the agent and vendor a day or so before the auction, and will depend to some extent on the amount of interest the agent has received prior to the auction date. If there has been very little interest, the buyer may decide to let the property go for less than originally anticipated in order to secure a sale, rather than risk failing at auction and having to start all over again on the open market. The reserve price is likely to be higher than the guide price.

TOP TIP

It is very important for vendors to be fully aware that the reserve price is the maximum figure they may end up selling for if the bidding does not go higher. It is a mistake to assume that the reserve price will be exceeded, so the figure should be the minimum you can afford to accept.

There are differences between setting the advertised selling price for a property being sold on the open market, and setting the guide price for an auction property. With open market sales, the advertised price is usually higher than the vendor anticipates achieving, and allows for a bit of bargaining by the buyer. In many cases, the advertised price is pitched to allow a convenience rounding down from, say, £45,750 to £45,000 to allow the buyer to feel he is getting a good deal. When selling at auction, however, the price quoted to prospective buyers is usually lower than the price the vendor hopes to achieve on the day and is pitched to attract as much interest as possible, so that on the day of the auction there are plenty of eager bidders in competition with each other, which pushes the final selling price up.

When agreeing (or not) to an agent's valuation on a property being sold on the open market, the vendor is able to compare his property with others of the same type, in the same area and on the market at the same time to make sure his idea of value matches the agent's. When considering the agent's valuation on an auction property however, it is more difficult for the vendor to come to his own conclusions unless he has some experience of auctions, which most of us do not. As a vendor it is useful to visit auctions to see for yourself how the process operates but, because most auction properties are highly individual (in terms of style and condition) it may not be possible to use this experience to compare prices because you are unlikely to come across a property similar to yours in every respect. The only thing you can do is research what the property is worth on the open market, then decide in view of this figure the minimum you are prepared to accept (the reserve) and hopefully achieve more on the day.

Many people believe that selling a property at auction is a desperate measure, only to be considered when the priority is to sell quickly, and the price achieved is a secondary issue. They believe that placing a property in an auction automatically reduces the attainable value and that the type of properties which go to auction are either derelict and only of interest to builders looking for a quick profit, or else mansions inviting excited bids through representatives on mobile telephones. The truth of the matter is that while a property sold at auction does need a realistic reserve to be sure of a sale, the right property can actually achieve a higher price at auction than it would on the open market.

Costs

The cost of selling at auction is slightly more expensive than selling on the open market because, whether or not the auction results in a successful sale, the vendor will be charged auction fees of around £250-500. On top of this comes the agent's commission which is usually the same as for selling under private treaty (around 2% of the final selling price) but this is not normally charged unless the auction results in a sale.

The legal conveyancing costs involved in selling at auction will be much the same as for selling on the open market. The solicitor acting for the vendor will need to prepare the contract in advance of the auction so that it is ready for signature on the day, so it is possible that the vendor may be asked to pay some moneys up front since if the auction is not successful the solicitor is unable to deduct his fee from the final sale proceeds in the usual way.

Promotion and conveyance

Properties going to auction are usually marketed in much the same way as properties being sold on the open market. The agent will view the property, give his impression as to the value, then prepare property details. These details will be sent to suitable applicants on the agent's mailing list and to those who respond to advertising. Advertising is often extensive and may encompass a wide range of publications. Advertising a property for auction focuses the attention of the buying public onto that particular property, and aims to attract the interest of buyers by intimation that the vendor intends to sell quickly and is not in a chain. Since advertising needs to be condensed into the short period between instruction and auction (often only 6 weeks), a property going to auction usually receives individual media coverage. Viewings will be arranged through the agent in the usual way, and since the marketing period is condensed, there may be a great many viewings in a short space of time.

DID YOU KNOW? *Selling agents dispatch far more sets of property details for an auction property than they do for a sale under private treaty.*

The conveyance and paperwork involved in an auction sale is much the same as for open market sales. A solicitor acting for the vendor will need to obtain the same information, complete the same forms and attend to details necessary to complete any conveyance, but the sequence is slightly different. For an auction sale, the vendor must arrange for the Contract to be ready for signature on the day of the auction to ensure that the buyer is legally committed to the purchase and does not have the opportunity to change his mind. The deposit is usually paid by the buyer on signature of the Contract. It is possible for the vendor to carry out a full search on his own property, and he may decide to do this so that buyers have to hand all the information they need to allow them to make a bid. (Forms LRC1 and Con.29, usually available from a solicitor or HMSO, will need to be supplied to the Council with a plan and the relevant fee, which is presently £48.). Alternatively, potential buyers will obtain a search through their own solicitors if time allows.

A buyer who intends to bid at auction will need to have arranged his funding in advance of the auction date. It is perfectly possible, contrary to popular belief, to get a mortgage on an auction property and lenders will approach the prospect of such funding in the same way as usual, except they will need a survey or valuation report before the auction so that they can decide on the amount of their formal offer of mortgage prior to the auction day. Lenders will not normally concern themselves with the amount the buyer actually pays for the property, but they will naturally have specified in the mortgage offer the amount they are prepared to lend. If the buyer decides to bid higher than the valuation, that is usually up to him, so long as he can meet the amount above the mortgage from his own funds.

Offers prior to auction

When selling agents receive an attractive bid prior to the auction date, they may recommend to the vendor that he accepts the bid and withdraws from the auction, but only if the buyer submits a good offer and is able to sign the Contract of Sale before the intended auction date. By withdrawing from the auction the vendor will avoid auction costs, and a sale may in this way be secured from a buyer would not ordinarily bid at auction. The agent will not normally withdraw a property from auction until the Contract of Sale is signed to avoid he possibility of the buyer backing out, and will allow the auction of the property to go ahead if the Contract cannot be prepared in time.

Occasionally, if several potential buyers have shown interest in a particular property and one of them makes an offer prior to auction, the selling agents will instigate a form of Dutch auction or telephone bidding. If, for example, the agents receive an offer from Mr First, they then contact Mrs Second, who has also shown an interest, explaining that an offer has been received. The amount should remain confidential, so on hearing this news Mrs Second can either disregard the property or make an offer in the hope that it is higher than Mr First's. If it is, the agents go back to Mr First with the bad news that a higher offer has been received, in response to which they hope Mr First will increase his offer. If so, the agents return to Mrs Second to see if she will better her offer, and so on until both potential buyers have their cards on the table and the highest price is reached. Understandably, this system is not popular with buyers.

Sometimes, when an agent has marketed a property for auction but a disappointing response gives him reason to doubt that it will succeed at auction, he may use another method to prompt a sale prior to the auction by inviting offers over a certain figure, to be received by a particular date. When the offers are received, the vendor has the option of accepting the offer from the buyer who has submitted the highest price and/or is in the best buying position. The successful buyer will then be contacted and the offer accepted on the condition that he is able to meet a deadline of, say, 14 days to sign a Contract of Sale. If the buyer is not in a position to sign the Contract within the deadline, the property will usually still go to auction, or alternatively the next best offer may be accepted in the same way if there is sufficient time prior to the auction for preparation of the Contract. From the vendor's point of view, he has saved his auction expenses and may well attract more offers in this way than he could expect to receive from people who might be unable or unprepared to bid at auction. A buyer who submits an offer under this system does not have any expenses if it is not accepted, so he may prefer to 'bid' for the property in this way rather than go to the trouble of attending an auction where his bid might not be accepted.

Agents

Not all estate agents handle auctions and, since there is more involvement by the agent in an auction sale than there is under private treaty, vendors should be careful to instruct an agent who is experienced not only in selling at auction generally, but in selling that particular type of property at auction. If the agent does not normally offer your type of property at the auctions he arranges, the audience could be wrong and, as already stated, a good auction needs plenty of competitive buyers in attendance.

An agent preparing for an auction sale will need to be more involved in active promotions and negotiations since he cannot afford to sit back and wait for buyers to come to him. The relatively short amount of time he has to market and advertise the property means he needs to gain interest quickly or else risk failure. Most agents who deal with auctions are Chartered Surveyors by profession, and the RICS will be able to supply a list of chartered surveyors in the area of vendors who want further information on auction procedures.

Vendors will be required to enter into a sole agency agreement for the period between the commencement of marketing and the auction date, during which time they undertake not to promote the property through any other agents. The sole agency agreement will usually extend to cover a short period, maybe a month, after the auction date if it was unsuccessful, to allow for a late bid from:

- any buyer who attended the auction but did not make a successful bid at the time; or
- any buyer who was not willing or sufficiently prepared to buy through the auction process.

Advantages of auction sales

The main advantage for vendors who decide to sell through an auction is that they can rest assured, once the highest bid has been accepted, that the property is bindingly sold and that completion of the transaction is not subject to breakdown of a chain or change of heart by the buyer. Once the contract is signed on the day of the auction there is finality to the transaction, which in the current market is very sought after.

DID YOU KNOW? *Estate agents report that properties for sale on the open market are commonly 'sold' two or three times before finally reaching a successful completion.*

Another plus for auction sales is that the timescale involved in selling at auction is usually very short, often only six weeks from commencement of marketing to the auction date, whereas properties for sale on the open market very often remain unsold for several months or even years. In a depressed housing market, many people only consider selling property because they have to, not because they want to, and in such cases they may not be able to afford the luxury of time. For vendors who are selling under time restraints, auctions offer the option of a quick sale.

When agents embark upon preparations for an auction sale they focus attention on a property, and tend to put extra effort into selling that particular property rather than simply meeting their general sales quota for the month. The agent's are also inclined to prepare distinctive written details for auction properties and the importance attached to auction sales may well mean that a property will command its own individual advertisement rather than be included among dozens of others.

DID YOU KNOW? *Buyers who are not reliant on selling a property before they can buy (or who have at least exchanged contracts on their own sale) are attracted to auctions by the prospect of avoiding chains.*

Disadvantages of auction sales

One of the main disadvantages for vendors selling at auction is the limited number of potential buyers who attend. Firstly, a buyer at auction will need to be in a position to sign a Contract of Sale on the day. To some extent this is not a disadvantage but an advantage, but vendors must remember that the number of buyers in this position is small compared to the overall market. The number of potential buyers who will even consider auctions as a way of buying property is further limited, partly because of the misconception that only cash buyers can buy through auctions, and partly because for some people the very idea of bidding at auction is not something they would consider doing. They imagine the process to be confusing and may even fear that a cough or sneeze during bidding could result in an unintentional purchase!

As a financial disadvantage, the vendor will incur auction expenses on top of his other selling costs whether or not the auction results in a sale, although for most people this is a small price to pay for knowing that, if the auction is a success, the buyer cannot pull out.

It can be seen then, that few obvious disadvantages face the vendor who elects to sell at auction. Although agents do not recommend experimenting with an auction on the assumption that the property can still be marketed on the open market if it fails, it really is still possible to sell the property on the open market if the auction fails. However, on a cautionary note, marketing a property after a failed auction can be difficult, because in effect you have shown your hand regarding price, which can result in a 'flat' selling period after the auction. Part of the reason for this is because auction properties are marketed at a low guide price. If the auction fails and the property is then advertised on the open market, the advertised selling price is likely to be much higher than the original guide price, making it appear that the value of the property has been inflated. The guide price might have been, for example, £50k-60k with the vendor expecting to achieve £65k-70k. Post auction the property is marketed at £72k with a view to dropping to around £70k; the vendor achieving much the same final price as he hoped to achieve at auction. However, buyers who receive the property details may notice this price irregularity and be reluctant to offer anything much above the original guide price. Happily, this scenario is not common because an auction usually attracts a different market to private treaty sales. While a buyer who requests details of properties going to auction will also get details of private treaty sales, a buyer who is on the agents normal mailing list probably won't be sent auction details.

In summary:

- Marketing agents must be experienced in auction sales in order to encourage competitive bidding on the day.
- The wrong type of property will not sell successfully at auction.
- Guide Price - Advertised price, designed to attract potential buyers.
- Reserve Price - Minimum selling price acceptable to the vendor.
- Usual selling costs are increased by auction expenses of around £250-500.
- Selling at auction requires advanced preparation of Contract by vendor's solicitor.
- Selling at auction requires advanced arrangement of valuation/survey, local searches and funding by the buyer and his solicitor.

- Advantages:
  - Sale on the day is binding.
  - Sale not subject to chain breakdown.
  - Shorter time taken from marketing to sale.
- Disadvantages
  - Limited market of buyers
  - Property for sale must be of a certain type
  - Higher selling costs

RECEIVING AN OFFER

Keeping your options open

Once a vendor receives an acceptable offer, it is a mistake for him to become complacent and assume that the property is unconditionally sold and that completion of the sale is now a mere formality. Many properties are 'sold' several times before completion is actually reached, normally as a result of a breakdown in the chain. It is most important for vendors to keep their property on the market until such time as the transaction is legally bound by exchange of contracts, because until such time the buyer can withdraw from the purchase for any reason without penalty, as can the vendor. Many buyers continue to view other properties even after placing an offer, and those who do so are clearly not committed to the purchase one hundred per cent. Since they are not legally or financially bound to the purchase until contracts are exchanged, they may wish to keep abreast of other property coming onto the market just in case something better comes along.

By keeping the property on the market even after receiving an offer, as a safeguard against being left high and dry by a buyer who changes his mind, the vendor is open to offers from other potential buyers, who can be kept 'in reserve' should the original sale fall through. Of course you cannot accept a further offer without pulling out of the original sale, but your agent can advise any other interested buyers that whilst the property is sold subject to contract, they will be contacted without delay if the property unexpectedly becomes available at a later date. In the unlikely event of a further offer being received which is higher than the first, tread carefully to establish that the new buyer is in just as good a buying position, if not better, than the original buyer, or risk losing both. Imagine the disappointment, if after receiving a better offer, you withdraw from the original sale but, having done so, the new buyer is subsequently unable to conclude the purchase for some reason. It is doubtful that the original buyer could be tempted back into the deal since he will probably have found somewhere else by then, and in any event will be wary of being let down again.

TOP TIP

Make sure your selling agents are aware that you wish them to continue promoting the property up until exchange of contracts, and that you are willing to accept viewings until that time.

Once an offer has been accepted, you may find that your buyer becomes quite friendly even if he seemed less than enthusiastic about the property during the viewing. It is quite often the case that an apparently eager applicant (one who delves into every cupboard and takes up a lot of time) is never heard from again, whilst the applicant who quickly and quietly looks around and only asks a few questions comes back the next day with an offer. Prospective buyers are often unenthusiastic during a viewing because they feel it would be foolish to show too much interest until a price has been agreed. After all, if they intend haggling over the price they do not want to appear too keen to buy the property at the start, but would rather give the impression that they can take it or leave it. Once the price has been agreed, you know the buyer is keen to buy, and he knows you know, so you can all relax.

But don't relax so much that you become careless and assume too much. Your buyer will almost certainly visit the property again; a second time to refresh his memory and maybe a third time to measure up for curtains etc.. Vendors often mistakenly assume that viewings arranged after an offer has been received are of no consequence. They believe that completion of the sale is a foregone conclusion, and that the buyer will not willingly back out of the purchase after making an offer, unless he is forced to do so by events outside his control. Unfortunately this is not always the case, and buyers have been known to simply change their minds when the property has disappointed them in some way during a subsequent visit (not so in Scotland [see below]). This can be put down to the fickle nature of buyers, but more commonly it is because vendors do not make sufficient effort to present the property well after an offer has been made, when in fact they should be just as keen to impress the buyer on subsequent visits as they were initially. The only change in the vendors approach to the buyer once an offer has been made, is that he (the vendor) may be more familiar with the buyer, expressing perhaps how the buyer was his first choice of new owner, being so suited to the property/area etc., and perhaps encouraging the buyer to feel 'at home' in the property by delaying him with a cup of coffee.

Offers in Scotland

In England there is not usually any pressure on buyers to submit their offer before a certain date, and if a buyer's first offer is not accepted he can submit another. In Scotland, however, agents often set a closing date by which 'blind bids' must be received (usually over a minimum asking price). Potential buyers have no idea at what level other buyers are bidding, and will not normally have the opportunity to submit a further offer if the first is not accepted. In both England and

Scotland there is no legal obligation for a vendor to accept the highest bid received, or in fact any bid, even though in Scotland prospective buyers will almost certainly have incurred costs in valuations fees before they are able to submit their offer.

In England an offer can hang in the balance for several weeks, if not months, between the time the offer is made and the point at which it becomes binding, i.e. when contracts are exchanged. In Scotland, whilst verbal acceptance of an offer is not binding, the time during which a buyer can withdraw his offer is usually much shorter. In most cases a formal acceptance of the offer is issued by the vendor's solicitor without delay, and as soon as the contract has been agreed in writing by the solicitors acting for both parties, the sale is binding. Because the buyer will already have carried out a valuation and arranged his mortgage before submitting an offer, the time between verbal offer and binding contract is usually less in Scotland than in England.

When an offer is received in Scotland, it usually comes from a buyer who has already arranged his finance and is in a position to proceed, so one buyer is not preferable over another in respect of his ability to conclude the purchase. However, a formal offer will contain contractual conditions, some of which may not meet with the vendor's approval (commonly these concern the date of entry, or inclusion of moveable items of furniture, so the contractual conditions may make one offer more attractive than another, and the question of whether or not a buyer is able to vary some of these conditions may determine whether his offer is accepted. The vendor will normally accept the highest offer received, if the contractual conditions are acceptable.

Chains

Sale and purchase transactions often fail to reach completion through no fault of the vendor or buyer, but simply because the 'chain' which both find themselves in breaks down. 'Chain' is the term used to describe a series of simultaneous transactions involving more than one buyer and seller, likening them to links in a chain. For example:

A   nothing to sell, is buying from B
B   selling to A, and buying from C

C   selling to B, and buying from D
D   selling to C, and buying a new home from builders.

If any one of the 'links' pulls out of the chain, the whole series of transactions can break down. If for example C withdraws because he cannot raise sufficient funds to buy from D, this leaves his buyer (B) with no property to buy, and the person he was buying from (D) with no buyer. In cases like this, the end of the chain is irrevocably broken because D will need to start all over again in his search for a buyer before he can purchase his new home. The bottom of the chain could be saved if B is able to find another property to buy quickly, but if he takes too long, his buyer (A) could decide to buy somewhere else. If the first-time buyer backs out (A), the chain could stay intact, but only if the rest of the links are prepared to wait for B to find another buyer.

This example of a fairly small chain with only four links would stand a good chance of success – the shorter the chain the less likelihood there is of a breakdown. Because so many failed transactions are the result of a broken chain, vendors should be aware of the buying position of a prospective buyer before accepting his offer.

Buying positions
Buyers submitting an offer to purchase usually fall into one of four categories, depending on their ability to proceed with the purchase without delay:

• Sold
The buyer's present property has been sold. This could mean that the buyer has actually moved out of his property into temporary accommodation, or alternatively that contracts have been exchanged and he is just waiting for the finalities to be concluded. Either way, the buyer has in effect disposed of his property and is in a position to purchase without delay. This type of buyer will probably drive a hard

bargain with the vendor of the property he decides to buy since he knows that few other buyers will be in as good a position as he, and that his custom is sought after. If the buyer is in temporary accommodation he may take a long time to finally decide on his choice of property since he is in no rush to move.

TOP TIP
The most favourable buyers are those who have exchanged contracts on their own property and are not prepared to move into temporary accommodation before buying again. Once a buyer is settled in temporary accommodation, he has no time restraints.

If the buyer has not actually moved out, but completion on his own sale is imminent, he may want assurance that the vendor of the property he selects to buy is going to move out quickly, so avoiding the type of timing mismatch which could force him to complete on his sale before he can complete on his purchase, necessitating a move into temporary accommodation. Accordingly, this type of buyer may be unwilling to involve himself in a long chain, so if the property you are buying is subject to a chain he may want assurances that you will complete quickly and move into temporary accommodation yourself if necessary, to fit in with his timescale, if your own purchase has not moved to completion. Think carefully before agreeing to this. If you move into temporary accommodation you will suffer the hassles of moving twice and possibly having to store furniture.

• Sold subject to contract

This buyer has received an offer on his own property but has yet to exchange contracts, so there is still an element of doubt over whether his sale is secure. This buyer is at the top of his chain so far. If he makes you an offer and you then buy from someone who is at the start of another chain (i.e. they are buying from someone who is buying from someone else and so on), you will be the middle link, effectively joining the two chains together. When considering an offer from a buyer who has sold subject to contract, it is wise to ask the agent to find out the nature of the chain the buyer is in, to see how long it is, and advise if the chain looks likely to break down. This type of buyer is not in a particularly strong position to negotiate the price with the vendor of his next property if he submits an offer in his present position. However, if he waits to exchange contracts on his own sale before submitting an offer, his bargaining position is much improved since he has then moved into the 'sold' category above.

- **On the market, but not yet sold**

This buyer is in exactly the same position as you. His buying status does not lend itself to bargaining over price, since it could take him longer to get an offer on his own property than it does for you to find another buyer. If an offer from this type of buyer is accepted, whilst taking the precaution of leaving the property on the market, you may find that other potential buyers may not be keen to compete with an existing offer under the inference that they must match or beat it.

- **First–time buyer**

Sadly there are not many of these about! The buyer has nothing to sell so he is in an excellent bargaining position, but vendors should ascertain whether or not this type of buyer has the necessary means of funding the purchase before accepting any offer, since first timers by definition have no experience of mortgage arrangements and may be over optimistic in estimating the amount their lender is prepared to advance. Because of the costs involved in applying for a local search, the solicitor acting for first–time buyers may not apply to the local authority for the search until his clients have received their mortgage offer, which could delay the transaction from the start. On a final note, first-time buyers are notoriously contrary and are apt to change their mind part way through a purchase. This may seem an unfair generalisation, but in many cases the observation is justified.

The agent's perspective

It is difficult for some inexperienced estate agents to appreciate the real value of their client's money when transactions involving hundreds of thousands of pounds pass through their hands every month. For this reason they may appear quick to advise a vendor to accept the first offer he receives, even if this is low, especially in a property market where offers are hard to come by. It is easy to see how an offer of £76k appears very reasonable to an agent when the asking price is £80k; after all, it's only a few thousand pounds off the asking price, and a few thousand pounds seems insignificant when the figures being discussed are so high. However, to the vendor, those thousands are real money, and represent next year's holiday or upgrading the family car.

Many people assume it is in the agent's interest to achieve the best possible price for his client, because the selling price directly determines the size of his commission, but this is not necessarily the case. Above all else, it is in the agent's best interest to remain solvent, and to do that he must achieve a satisfactory turnover of sales. The agent must therefore balance his reputation for achieving good selling prices, against disposing of properties quickly in order to keep the agency in business. As far as his commission is concerned, it is often in his best interest to recommend acceptance of a low offer, even though his commission will be reduced. Take for example the situation where a vendor receives an offer of £78,000 which is £2,000 less than he expected. The normal agency commission on the £2,000 under discussion is only about £40 (i.e. 2%), whereas the actual commission payable to the agent if the sale goes ahead at £78,000 is £1,560. Obviously it is not worth the agent losing a sale for the sake of £40, so it is in the agent's best interests if the offer is accepted. Most agents value their reputation and achieve the best price they can for their clients, but for some the risk of losing a commission altogether if the buyer backs out of the deal can blur the obligation to a client.

At end of the day, the vendor is the only person who can decide whether or not an offer is acceptable. The agent's job is to negotiate between buyer and vendor until agreement is reached and everyone is happy, and for the most part they do this very well, especially when considering that they are in a 'no win' situation. If the agent recommends accepting an offer which is low he makes the buyer happy but not the vendor, whilst if he recommends refusing a low offer he disappoints the buyer and the vendor is still not happy because no sale has been achieved. Either way, the agent cannot please all of the people all of the time.

Surveys and valuations – what to expect

The very mention of a survey or valuation is enough to strike fear into the heart of many a confident vendor, especially if there are some known faults in the property, and some vendors go to extraordinary lengths to conceal defects which they fear will 'fail' a survey. Unfortunately, carefully placed furniture designed to hide a damp spot rarely foils a good surveyor, and modern equipment such a damp meters aid detection. However, although it may appear that surveyors inspect a property with grim determination, doggedly persevering until something wrong is found, they are usually only concerned with defects which affect the value of a property, not those which affect the general appearance. So, whilst a survey or valuation report will comment on damp and decay in the fabric of a building, a cosmetic flaw is unlikely to raise any eyebrows.

DID YOU KNOW?   *Under the Property Misdescription Act (1991) there is no obligation to disclose that a previous survey has been carried out on a property, or the results of that survey. However, it is an offence to make a statement which is misleading because it does not tell the whole truth by omission of an unfavourable detail, and answers to any questions must be truthful and not equivocal.*

There are several types of survey, ranging from the basic valuation (insisted upon by banks and building societies before they issue a mortgage offer), to full surveys which will cost the buyer dearly. The type of survey is usually at the discretion of the buyer, although it is possible that a bank or building society may only agree to lend after an in-depth survey if an initial valuation report reveals some aspects which require further investigation.

DID YOU KNOW?   *The owner of a property on which a valuation or survey is carried out will not normally have sight of the report, even though it may be used by the buyer to negotiate the price*

In most cases the valuation or survey is carried out after the buyer has submitted an acceptable offer and before his formal mortgage offer is obtained (except in Scotland – see below). The agents dealing with the sale will usually contact the vendor to arrange an appointment for the surveyor to conduct his inspection, and while the vendor might prefer to be present during the inspection it is not imperative and most agents will stand in for the vendor if the appointment is not convenient. The vendor does not normally contribute to the valuation process, and the surveyor will usually go about his business without direction or discussion. The vendor is not normally required to supply guarantees for repairs or improvements to the surveyor during his inspection, since the buyer's solicitor will normally be the one to ask for such information.

There are basically four different types of 'survey' which could be carried out on a property:

• **Lender's Valuation Report**

This is primarily a valuation of the property to ensure that there is adequate security for the loan (or mortgage) being made on it. It is used by lenders to gauge the money they could recover, should they have to dispose of the property, so the value the surveyor puts on a property will need to at least equal the amount the buyer needs to raise by mortgage. The surveyor will not normally lift floorboards or delve too deeply into the fabric of the property during a valuation, but he may advise obtaining specialist reports if he feels this is appropriate. He will primarily report on 'essential repairs' which, left uncorrected, would cause further damage to the property, and may report on specific aspects of the property's condition which has led to his opinion of the value, although any specific defects mentioned will only tend to be those which reflect on the value. Other defects, while they may involve costs to the buyer, may not be mentioned.

Most banks and building societies insist on obtaining a Valuation Report before granting a mortgage on a property, at the expense of the buyer. Many banks and building societies have an list of 'approved' surveyors who they use regularly, so it is usually the lender who appoints the surveyor.

DID YOU KNOW?   *Although the buyer may be given a copy of a Valuation Report, it is obtained for the lenders and belongs to them, so the buyer may have no recourse if the report is inconclusive.*

• **Private Survey Report**

Most commonly used in Scotland, this Report is commissioned by the buyer and is paid for and owned by him. It is carried out by a chartered surveyor who has an obligation to his client (the buyer) to take reasonable professional care over its preparation. The report will almost certainly give the surveyor's considered opinion on the property's value, and this is usually acceptable for lenders considering a mortgage application. This type of report will often, when assessing value, comment on current market conditions which may affect the selling price of the property, and the buyer will usually have the opportunity to discuss the price and other matters with the surveyor and may ask to be present during the inspection.

The extent of the surveyor's comments on the condition of a property will usually be determined by available access, since fitted carpets and fitted furniture may restrict access to inspect floorboards and sections of wall etc.. If the surveyor is unable to get access to certain aeas of the property his report will usually say so. If the buyer has a specific query about the property, he will be able to discuss it with the surveyor.

• Home Buyers' Survey and Valuation

A combination of valuation and survey, this is more detailed than a basic valuation so vendors can expect the surveyor to make a more thorough inspection. The surveyor will comment on both the value and condition of the property and will inspect for defects where access allows. This type of report is usually prepared on a pre-printed form so it does not allow the same level of flexibility as a Building Survey for reporting on specific enquiries. This level of inspection is probably the most commonly used by buyers.

• Building Survey

This type of report is the most extensive, and is sometimes the second step after a valuation or home buyer's report if the surveyor recommends more detailed information is needed before the purchase goes ahead. The report is usually commissioned by the buyer and is expensive, but it's advantage is that it allows the buyer the opportunity to raise any specific queries with the surveyor. Minor defects such as loose door fittings or cracked glass are not usually mentioned, but the general condition of the property will be appraised, including:

- foundations
- walls, both external and internal
- internal flooring and ceilings
- windows, doors and external joinery
- facia and soffit boards
- pipes, drains and gutters
- roof
- chimney stacks

TOP TIP

The vendor's selling agents may not be aware of the type of survey the buyer or his lender have arranged. If the vendor wishes to know what to expect, he can ask the agents to ascertain how long the surveyor will need to be at the property to conduct his investigation. If he needs about an hour, the surveyor will probably be carrying out a Valuation. A building survey can take several hours, so anything in between is probably a home buyer's report.

Services will be commented on where visible, and though they probably won't be physically tested by the surveyor, specialists in heating, drainage etc. may be called in to supply additional reports. The surveyor will often request details of any charges relating to the property, along with details of boundaries, and he will usually comment on any building repairs or alterations which could affect the property.

The valuation or survey does not only directly affect whether or not the buyer goes ahead with the purchase, it also determines the amount a lender is prepared to lend and can affect the ultimate selling price if the buyer uses the report as a bargaining tool. Once a buyer has details of the property and its condition, he is in a position to haggle over the price and may expect the vendor to make a reduction in consideration of any necessary repairs, even though the selling agent's initial marketing valuation will have taken these into account. It is therefore important for vendors to do what they can to ensure the survey goes as smoothly as possible.

• Correct any maintenance faults you are aware of, and can reasonably afford. It may not be practical to enter into the cost of major repairs, or cost effective to do so (see also Chapter 4, Improvements), so care should be taken to decide which defects will cost relatively little to repair but may affect a valuation or survey, as opposed to those defects which are expensive to repair but are unlikely to warrant a mention in the report. Some repairs can be carried out for very little cost and without going to the expense of employing people to do the work for you, for example giving the internal or external window frames an overhaul and repaint. Other repairs which require the employment of specialists or which lead to much disruption and redecorating, may not be worth the expense.

• Obtain quotes for the repair of any faults known to you which may come to light in a survey or valuation report. If allowance for these faults has not been fairly reflected in the asking price and made apparent to the buyer before he submits his offer, be prepared for the buyer to reduce his offer to take account of any necessary repairs revealed by the surveyor. By obtaining quotes in anticipation of price negotiations, you will be in a position to discuss fairly and openly the cost of any necessary work, so that you are not bargained down on price any further than you need to be.

• Make sure the property looks well cared for. The surveyor is a professional and will be looking for faults. However, while he will disregard dust on skirting boards as irrelevant as long as the timber is sound, he will notice the overall condition of the property which could affect his opinion of the value.

In some cases the valuation figure in a surveyor's report may be less than the buyer's offer, which could result in the buyer reducing his offer through necessity, if he is borrowing a large proportion of the purchase price. The lender is unlikely to lend more than the valuation figure, so the buyer may not be able to make up the difference between the valuation figure and the amount needed to fund the purchase. In any event, the buyer will be guided by the surveyor on value, and will naturally not want to pay more for the property than his surveyor considers it is worth.

DID YOU KNOW?   *The surveyor should have a good knowledge of market prices and will sometimes be better able to judge a property's value than the selling agents. Unlike the agents, he is not under pressure from the vendor to meet any price aspirations, so gives a totally honest valuation.*

If the buyer will not proceed with the sale because the survey report has valued the property lower than the offer figure, the vendor may decide to accept a lower offer, since any subsequent valuations carried out for future buyers will probably reach a similar conclusion. On the other hand, it could be that the buyer is simply using the report to push for a better deal, and is not seriously considering dropping out of the purchase if his reduced offer is not accepted. The vendor and his agents will need to carefully ascertain which is the case, and act accordingly.

Vendors sometimes suffer frustration and stress when their buyer is slow to arrange the survey on their property, and often fear that the buyer is not serious about the purchase because of the delay. If the buyer must sell his present property before he can proceed with the purchase, he could be waiting for the results of his buyer's survey before going to the expense of paying for a survey on the next purchase. He will want to avoid spending money on a survey or anything else if there is a possibility that his own buyer might drop out. This can lead to delays because his lender is not in a position to grant the formal mortgage offer until the valuation or survey report has clarified the property's value and condition.

The surveyor has two main functions when submitting his report. Firstly, he clarifies that the property is in the condition it appears to be to the untrained eye, and brings defects to the attention of the buyer and lender. Secondly, the surveyor gives his opinion on the value of the property, and in this way he gives the lender and buyer an indication of the sum the property could raise on disposal, should the need arise.

Valuations in Scotland

When a buyer instructs a surveyor in Scotland, he usually does so before submitting an offer. Since the offer may not be accepted, this can lead to a buyer going to the expense of commissioning surveys on several different properties before his offer on one is finally accepted. However, on the plus side, the buyer has vital knowledge on the condition of the property before deciding on the amount he wants to offer, because he then knows, allowing for the cost of any repairs, what the property is worth to him. The surveyor's report will give an indication of the property's value, but this is not a guarantee that the bid will be successful at that level, since the report is not able to take account of competition for the purchase which could result in other bids being higher. Conversely a buyer may submit an offer based on the valuation figure, when the vendor would in fact have been willing to accept a lower offer, especially if the property has attracted very little interest and no closing date has been set..

Negotiating the price

In considering whether to accept a particular offer, the vendor probably has in mind a minimum sum he can accept, and a higher sum which is a bit hopeful. Price negotiations demand a skill few of us are blessed with, but obviously it is important not to drop to the minimum figure too quickly which will leave no room for further negotiations.

The offer a buyer first suggests will be the lowest he thinks he can get away with. The vendor may accept this offer if he feels it is fair and reasonable, and assuming it is within his minimum requirements. Alternatively, the vendor may not immediately agree to the offer, asking instead for time to consider it, whatever it is, establishing that he is not 'desperate' to sell at any price. It can be dangerous to play this game for too long since the buyer could be dissuaded from the purchase if the vendor appears hostile to negotiations. If, after consideration, the vendor decides that the offer is not acceptable, he can then instruct the selling agent to do what he is being paid for, namely to negotiate on his behalf. It may be that some compromise can be achieved on fixtures and fittings which both buyer and vendor can live with. Perhaps the buyer will agree to raise his offer on the understanding that the garden shed and greenhouse are included in the sale, or perhaps the vendor may agree to the original offer on the understanding that the purchase will not now include certain items which he had previously intended to include. The vendor will be required to supply a list of fixtures and fittings to his solicitor once the transaction is underway, and this will clarify which items are included in the purchase price and which are not.

After the survey or valuation, the buyer may reduce his original offer. When the buyer has sight of the surveyor's report he may reconsider the property's worth based on whatever defects the surveyor has unearthed. If the defects were apparent in the estate agent's details, the vendor can argue that the asking price reflected them. If the defects were not apparent, the vendor should be in a position to supply estimates for the repairs and then negotiate, perhaps coming to some agreement over the costs involved.

Occasionally a buyer will reduce his offer at the last moment before exchange of contracts, after a great deal of time and effort has been put into moving the transaction to that stage. It would be unwise to assume that this ploy will necessarily be a bluff and that the buyer will not really pull out of the deal if the price is not reduced. The buyer may in fact be doing exactly what his own buyer is doing, leaving him with insufficient funds from his own sale to meet the purchase price. However, a buyer who has spent money on a survey, mortgage application, local searches, solicitor's fees etc. is unlikely to withdraw at the last minute unless there is no alternative. Unlikely, but not unheard of, so vendors will need to establish the buyer's position before deciding whether or not to call his bluff.

DID YOU KNOW?   *In England properties are marketed at a higher price than the vendor expects to achieve. In Scotland, however, the marketing price is usually the minimum the vendor is prepared to accept and offers are invited over that amount.*

Lies, all lies
As a final word on selling a property, from initial promotion to the point of receiving an offer, it is depressing but none the less true that throughout the process, people often lie. They may not be intent on deceit and may simply be vague or unwilling to divulge information which is no one else's business, but vendors should be aware that everyone is doing it!

- Applicants lie to agents about their buying position.
- Buyers lie to vendors about what they think of the property,

their reason for moving and their financial position.
- Agents lie to applicants about the amount of interest a property is attracting.
- Vendors lie to applicants about the condition of the property, how long they have lived there and the neighbourhood.
- Vendors lie to applicants about the amount of interest their property has attracted.
- Buyers lie to vendors and selling agents about progress with their own sale and how quickly they can move.
- Agents lie to applicants about how long a property has been for sale.
- Vendors lie to agents about their sale aspirations, assuming the minimum they say they need will be the maximum they finally get.

In summary:

- Keep the property on the market once an offer has been received, allowing for the possibility of an aborted sale.
- Buyers often visit the property they are buying after submitting an offer, and can be put off if the property is not presented so well for subsequent visits.
- A buyer's ability to progress quickly with a purchase will depend on his buying position, i.e. whether he is involved in a chain transaction or not.
- Surveys and valuation reports are primarily used to determine the value of the property and its condition. There are several types:
  - Valuation report
  - Home buyer's report and valuation
  - Building survey
- The property should be prepared with care prior to survey or valuation.

PAPERWORK AND LEGALITIES

Conveyancing - what is it?

The considerable amount of paperwork involved in 'selling' a property, sends most of us scurrying to the nearest solicitor who will deal with the legal aspects of transferring ownership of the property from one person to another on our behalf. The term generally used to describe such a transfer is 'conveyance', which literally means 'a transfer of the legal title to property [or] the document effecting such a transfer'. This basically means drawing up and submitting certain documents for signature, which legally take a property out of the ownership of one person (or persons) and into the ownership of someone else.

Choosing a legal representative

NOTE: For the purpose of simplicity, the term 'solicitor' has been used in reference to a legal representative and encompasses Licensed Conveyancers as well as solicitors.

Solicitors are not the only experts in the field of conveyancing, and in 1985 an Act of parliament created an alternative by introducing a new body of people to deal with conveyancing matters in the form of Licensed Conveyancers, who are not necessarily solicitors but rather a parallel profession specialising in the legalities of buying and selling property. The Society of Licensed Conveyancers (Tel: 0181-681-1001) are able to advise on licensees in different areas. As regards fees, there is usually little difference between the charges made by licensed conveyancers and solicitors

If you already use a solicitor, or know of someone who comes recommended, all well and good. If you have used a particular firm in the past and were pleased with their services, you will be best advised to stick with them. It is not that good solicitors are hard to find, most of them are honest, hard working people, but building up a good relationship with your solicitor will be invaluable if you need clarification on any part of the conveyance, or if you wish him to make special enquiries on your behalf.

TOP TIP

Consult your bank or building society when searching for a suitable solicitor since they may be able to recommend firms who have proved themselves efficient
in past dealings.

There is no need to limit your choice of solicitor to a local firm. In these days of modern office technology, and in order to keep costs down, most information handled by a solicitor will be sent through the post (document exchange) or by fax, or is dealt with over the telephone, so it is not necessary for the solicitor to be located near the property. This is useful if you are selling and buying simultaneously in different parts of the country when there is no reason why one solicitor cannot handle both transactions. In fact it is desirable for one solicitor to act for you in both transactions because the amount of correspondence will be reduced and generally speaking the fewer people involved, the less chance of delays.

If you need legal assistance with other matters directly or indirectly connected to the property sale, possibly the property is an inheritance or you are selling because of divorce, you might prefer to have all matters dealt with by the same person, in which case you will need to engage a solicitor, rather than an licensed conveyancer who will only be able to deal with matters relating to the property sale. However, be sure to check that your solicitor is willing and able to handle matters in addition to the conveyancing, since nowadays solicitors are more used to specialising in one field.

If turning to the telephone directory to make your choice, be sure to speak to at least three different firms to get an idea of the fees they charge, since these can vary enormously.

Costs

The conveyancing charges made by a solicitor for his time and attention are usually based on the value of the property, so when you obtain a quote the solicitor will ask for the selling price. Although most solicitors charge much the same fee whether handling a sale or purchase, the additional costs involved in a purchase will be higher than for a sale, including such items as search fees, land registry charges and stamp duty.

Always agree the fee with your chosen solicitor before instructing him to start work on your behalf. Many vendors are out of touch with current conveyancing charges and, having failed to obtain a quote prior to instruction, they receive a nasty shock when the solicitor deducts his fee from the sale proceeds. When confirming the fee for conveyancing, it is useful to ask your solicitor to clarify any other costs you can expect to encounter, especially when buying as well as selling, which will help you to budget for the inevitably high demand on your resources. See page 181 for an example of a quote.

RANDSFELL SOLICITORS

Mr & Mrs Vendor
12 Lyndale Avenue
Stoke Lyndon
Warwickshire

Dear Mr & MrsVendor

**Re: Sale of 12 Lyndale Avenue and
       Purchase of Lake Cottage**

I write to confirm my quotation in connection with
your above sale and purchase, as follows:

Legal fees in connection with sale @ 50,000	295.00
Legal fees in connection with purchase @ 54,000	295.00
	590.00
VAT @ 17.5%	103.25
Local Search Fees	56.00
Office copy entries	14.00
Land Registry fees	140.00
Other searches (estimate)	5.00
Telegraphic transfer fee	30.00
Total	938.25

I trust this is satisfactory.

Yours sincerely

'Cut price' conveyancing could soon be coming to an end in England and Wales if the Governing Council of the Law Society concludes plans discussed in December 1995 which may force solicitors to increase the fees they charge. The move follows concerns that some conveyancers have been cutting corners in order to offer cheaper deals. Many leading solicitors now believe that competition is forcing conveyancing fees down to a level where solicitors can no longer afford to devote the necessary time and resources to adequately handle the conveyance. This gives rise to problems, particularly when a solicitor handles an unusual property which needs more time and attention than his 'cut price' quote will allow, and there have been claims that cut price deals have resulted in some solicitors failing to gain adequate information for clients purchasing a property, including checking that planning consents have been granted.

Wide consultation in the profession will decide whether to set quality standards in return for compulsory minimum fees in an effort to stamp out cut price conveyancing, and if this goes ahead consumers can expect conveyancing fees to rise.

DID YOU KNOW? *Cut price conveyancing can mean low grade staff and no personal attention. A general quote will usually only cover a standard type job, so costs are likely to increase if peculiarities are encountered.*

Working with your solicitor

You may feel, especially if your property has been on the market for some time, that it is not worth instructing or even selecting a solicitor until such time as you receive a firm offer of purchase. In fact, it is often useful to provisionally instruct a solicitor before receiving an offer so that you are in a position to get matters moving without delay when you do find a buyer. In this way you and your solicitor can work together to gather information and prepare some of the documentation in advance, which will save time later.

Years ago, solicitors visited properties when they were instructed to handle a conveyance, and personal observations made them better able to anticipate any problems which could arise. Nowadays however, because of cost and time restrictions, solicitors no longer physically see the properties, and to some extent are working in the dark with no first hand knowledge. Because of this, they must rely on their client to advise them of any peculiarities relating to the property which may not be disclosed in the paperwork, i.e. a right of way over the garden, and vendors should always make sure their solicitor has a copy of the written property details produced by the selling agents. A good solicitor will go through the agency details carefully and, hopefully, spot anything which could present problems or raise queries. For example, this could be something which comes to light in the agent's directions on how to find the property, mentioning that "access is obtained down a private road.". You may not see this as a problem, and it may not be one, but your solicitor will need to clarify whether or not the road is 'private' only in a graphic description and has in fact been adopted by the council or, if it really is private property, ascertain what rights you have over it and who owns it or is responsible for repair and maintenance. The agency details should include details of boundaries etc., but anything which you discover has been omitted but which directly or indirectly affects the property should be brought to the attention of your solicitor as soon as possible; preferably before the buyer or his solicitor notices it!

Some solicitors, mercifully few though they are, do not obtain necessary information from their clients until the buyer's solicitor demands such information. Similarly, many vendors do not anticipate what information will be requested of them, and often find themselves desperately hunting for various documents which have, by that time, become urgent. A vendor may have reason to contact his landlord (in the case of a leasehold property), or need to request documents from his insurance company, and since it could take some time to receive a reply, this type of stress and delay can only be avoided if vendor and solicitor have all the necessary information to hand, including:

- Documents for the last three years relating to service charges and ground rent (with the latest receipt) if the property is leasehold.
- In Scotland, details of any feu duty or similar payment, e.g. annual communal ground maintenance, and the latest receipt. Where there is a property factor, the latest account should be supplied and the solicitor advised whether the factor holds a 'float' which needs to be repaid to the vendor on completion of the sale.
- The builder's NHBC guarantee or equivalent if the property is less than 10 years old.
- Planning permission / building regulation consents.
- Guarantees for repairs i.e. damp proofing, wood treatment, double glazing, cavity insulation.
- A copy of the estate agency details.
- Details of buildings insurance.

Even before receiving an offer for the property, a vendor can obtain from his solicitor the Property Information Form and Fixtures and Fittings form, and complete these in readiness. These forms are usually sent to the buyer's solicitor with the contract and can be dispatched more quickly if the forms are already to hand and not spending several days in the post to you, then several more days in the post going back to your solicitor.

As soon as an acceptable offer is received for your property, you will be asked to supply the buyer with the name and address of your legal representative and, if you are taking out another mortgage, many lenders will be unable to process the loan application without details of your solicitor. It is therefore prudent to decide which firm you want to use before receiving an offer, to avoid any unnecessary delays at the start.

TOP TIP

Clarify the name of the particular solicitor who will be handling your conveyancing, and always ask to speak to him or her personally. Do not accept being dealt with by whoever happens to be in the office when you call – they will not be as aware of your case or any particular concerns you have.

It is worth mentioning at this point the folly of not keeping your solicitor informed, or worse still, attempting to keep him in the dark. Vendors have been known to avoid divulging to their solicitor something which they fear could be construed as detrimental to the property, in the hope that by the time the buyer becomes aware of the problem he will be emotionally or financially committed to proceeding with the purchase regardless. This is not an advisable practice and, quite apart from the moral viewpoint, it rarely results in a positive outcome. Litigation over property matters is extremely expensive and complex, frequently involving surveyors and often the solicitors as third parties. In any event, in practice the decision whether or not to proceed under such circumstances is not only in the hands of the buyer, since the lender will probably refuse to fund the purchase if there is doubt cast on whether the property has a 'good and marketable title', no matter how keen the buyer is to proceed. Almost all lenders insist on having a valuation or survey carried out on a property prior to approving a loan for the purchase, and the surveyor's report will bring to light anything which could reflect badly on the purchase. At the end of the day, if the property does not represent a sound investment, the lender will not consent to the loan.

In some cases, a property can be wrongly construed as having a problem in the eyes of the buyer, but because the vendor's solicitor is not told of the situation in advance he is not in a position to refute it. For example, a property may be situated on a flood plain, but the problem of flooding was in fact been rectified some time ago by a river diversion or new flood defences. If the vendor's solicitor is aware of the situation he can supply the necessary information to the buyer's solicitor in order to clarify the situation, and so stop the matter ever being raised as a problem. A road widening scheme may be a positive advantage to a property's location, but if a buyer only sees the proposal in outline from the planning department, it could put him off. If he has explanations from your solicitor, his mind will be put at rest.

Speeding up the system

In most cases, the sale of a property follows the simple process of a vendor supplying various items of information to, and then swapping certain documents with, a buyer. The process is not complicated but relies on a lot of people (vendor, solicitors, estate agents, land registry, buyer, lenders etc.) to supply documents and information, so delays, when they occur, often do so simply because of the sheer number of individuals involved. Postal delays are also responsible for holding up the process – when you consider that a document may need to go from the vendor to his solicitor, from the vendor's solicitor to the buyer's solicitor, from the buyer's solicitor to the buyer and then possibly to the mortgagees and their solicitors and then back, it is easy to see how a single document can easily take a fortnight to be dealt with. If there are a lot of issues which need clarification or enquiries which need replies, this adds up to a lot of fortnights.

There are several forethoughts a vendor can employ to speed up the process:

- Supply your solicitor with details of your lender so that the deeds can be obtained prior to securing a sale.
- Always use the postcode when returning documents and make sure everyone who may need to write to you has yours. If you have a FAX machine, give out the number.
- Confirm with your solicitor the selling price and details of the selling agents as soon as an acceptable offer is received.
- Local searches can be obtained by the vendor on his own property, and if these are submitted to the buyer's solicitor with the contract this can save around 10 days. However, searches are only valid for a set period so if the property does not sell quickly they will need to be done again. At a cost of around £50 you will need to be sure they are not wasted. Do not necessarily expect your buyer to refund the cost.
- When documents are sent to you for signing, always return them promptly and make sure you have done exactly what has been asked of you, e.g. that your signature has been correctly witnessed.

If you are buying a subsequent property:

- Mortgage funding can take time to arrange, so speak with the mortgage officer at your bank or building society as soon as you know you will be moving, and do not delay in supplying them with the information they request. Many lenders will agree lending to a figure in principle, provided the property when found comes up to valuation. There is little point in getting things ready for a speedy sale if you allow your next purchase to hold up the proceedings, unless you are intending to move into temporary accommodation in the interim.

- If you have a specific enquiry, perhaps regarding clarification of a boundary, raise this early on. Your solicitor (who will not normally see the property) may be unaware of the problem and may need to apply for information from the vendor, through the land registry or similar, and it could take time for this information to be supplied back to him

Not all delays can be circumvented, but when you consider that around 90% of conveyancing is concerned with trying to obtain information and agree dates, you begin to see how being organised and well prepared can help speed up the process.

The legal process

Assuming a freehold property being sold in England or Wales (the conveyancing system in Scotland is different and is dealt with in the next chapter), the vendor will encounter various documents in need of signature and approval, while behind the scenes his solicitor and the buyer's solicitor will be beavering away at the conveyancing process, awaiting replies to questions/searches, which will eventually result in the (hopefully smooth) transfer of property.

• Fixtures and fittings

One of the first documents you will receive from your solicitor is a printed form asking which fixtures, fittings and contents you are leaving in the property you are selling. You will probably have agreed with your buyer whether or not you are leaving such things as the garden shed, wall lights, carpets etc. but he will want to be reassured that you will actually leave what he thinks you will leave. This form should be completed with care, then returned to your solicitor, who will then send it to your buyer's solicitor. It is worth keeping a copy of this form so that on the day of moving out:

- you only take what you said you would take; and
- you don't leave anything behind which is not included in the sale.

• Searches

It is possible for the vendor to apply for the local search on his own property to speed up the transaction. This was a useful option for vendors when property was selling quickly, because in those days it didn't take long to find a buyer. In addition, local authorities were under such high pressure from demand, that it was not unusual for a search to take up to three months to come back. However, the search is only valid for a limited time, so unless you are confident of securing a sale within the validity period, it will be out of date. It is more usual for the purchaser's solicitor to apply for the local search, but at a cost of around £50 he may not want to go to this expense until he obtains mortgage funding, which can commonly cause a 3 week delay.

The local search application is sent to the local authority and discloses such things as whether the property is a listed building and local road-widening schemes, although not everything will be marked against the property. The search will also show planning consents and building regulation consents relating to the property, so if your property has undergone alterations which required planning or building consents you will need to supply these documents to your solicitor since the buyer's solicitor will request them. Replies to local searches take around 10 days to be received from local authorities.

The buyer's solicitor will also apply to the Land Registry to see if there are any changes on the land registry.

DID YOU KNOW? *Applying for searches on a property is a simple matter – it is the ancillary matters, the practical nuts and bolts which have an effect on the ability of the vendor to sell the property, and which hold things up, e.g. obtaining damp/rot certificates.*

• The contract

Your solicitor will write out a contract of sale, identifying the vendor and purchaser and listing any conditions, such as the amount of deposit the buyer will supply on exchange of contracts. A copy of this Contract will then be sent to the purchaser's solicitor (unsigned, of course) for his approval. As already discussed, if you supply your solicitor with documents such as NHBC Certificate, planning consents, Fixtures and Fittings and Property Information forms, these can be sent to the buyer's solicitor with the draft Contract to save time.

• Preliminary Information Forms
These were previously known as Preliminary Enquiry forms. Your purchaser's solicitor (via yours) will send a standard form requesting 'preliminary information', which you will be asked to complete and return. The information requested will concern who owns particular boundary fences, whether there have been any disputes which could affect the new owner and other questions concerning rights of access, notices, restrictions, guarantees, services, etc., etc. You are required to answer these questions truthfully or, if you are not sure of the answer, say so. You may have already obtained one of these standard Forms from your own solicitor and returned it to him, completed, to save time.

• Exchange of Contracts
Once the preliminary information has been supplied by you, and the contract has been approved, a copy contract (signed by you) is despatched to your buyer's solicitor, and the identical copy contract which has already been sent to the buyer's solicitor for approval and signature is returned to your solicitor. This is the exchange of contracts, and once this takes place the agreement to buy and sell is binding. This is also usually the point at which a date for completion is agreed, so you can make arrangements for removals, postal redirection, disconnection of services etc..

At the time contracts are exchanged, the buyer becomes liable to pay a deposit which used to be 10% but is now more often 5%. It is common to use the deposit received on a sale as a deposit on a purchase, so if you are purchasing as well as selling, your solicitor will use the deposit the buyer pays to you as the deposit on your next property, but this must be agreed by all parties if you are in a chain. For example:

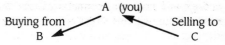

In the short chain shown above, C is buying your home and you in turn are buying from B. C, as a first-time buyer, will need to raise the necessary funds for the deposit, which his solicitor will send to your solicitor. You will not usually need to supply funds personally to pay the deposit to B because your solicitor will bank your buyer's cheque in his client account and then write a cheque to B's solicitor for the deposit you are liable for. The exception to this might be if B is demanding a higher deposit amount than your buyer is paying, maybe because 5% of B's selling price is higher than 5% of your selling price. In this case you may be required to make up the difference.

In some cases the deposit from C is paid directly to B if there is agreement from all parties. This makes little difference to you, since the amount you would receive from C would normally be indirectly paid over to B anyway. If you were not purchasing a further property, the deposit from C would simply be held by your solicitor and then paid to you together with the balance of payment for the property.

After exchange of contracts, the buyer becomes liable for the property he is purchasing, although he has no right of occupation. The property is at the purchaser's risk, so in the unlikely event it burns down between exchange of contracts and completion, the buyer is still required to proceed with the purchase, so it is usual for him to insure the building. Many mortgage companies automatically insure properties on which they are lending, and the buyer's solicitor may as a matter of course notify the lender on the date of exchange so that the property is covered. However, if the buyer is not borrowing or is arranging his own insurance he must insure from the moment the contracts are exchanged.

The period between exchange of contracts and completion used to be around 4 weeks, but is now more commonly 2 weeks. If there is a chain which has taken a long time to put together, the period could be even shorter because buyers and vendors will not want any further delays.

• Discharging the mortgage

Your lender will be asked to supply a redemption figure on your existing mortgage, showing the amount required to discharge the mortgage on completion of the sale – in other words how much you still owe. Your existing mortgage must be repaid when you sell your property, and in most cases your solicitor will deal with the redemption. However, if another separate solicitor is employed by your lender to deal with the redemption, you may well be asked to pay the lender's legal fee as well.

Some lenders penalise early repayment of mortgages by charging a mortgage redemption fee which can be equivalent to several months interest. This usually only applies if the mortgage is paid off within the first years and the mortgage rate was fixed at the start, if the mortgage was discounted, or if there was a 'cash-back' arrangement. This fee can often be avoided by taking out a new mortgage with the same lender on your next property, but the sale and subsequent purchase may need to be conducted within a limited space of time.

In cases of negative equity, i.e. the property being sold is worth less than the mortgage on it, some banks and building societies allow lenders with negative equity to sell their existing property, then buy another and take the negative equity with them, i.e. transfer the mortgage in negative equity onto the new property. This allows the opportunity to move to a cheaper property, so reducing the amount of the loan, although the negative equity will remain the same. If you are selling your property for this reason you must sell and buy simultaneously because there cannot be a time, however short, when there is no property on which the funding is secured. There are various stipulations made by lenders in cases of negative equity, so you will need to speak to your lender to see whether or not you comply with their conditions. Bear in mind also that moving home will cost money in fees etc. and since you will probably not be able to borrow money for this, you will need some cash to cover moving costs.

• **Requisitions on title**

Your solicitor will be asked to confirm that there have been no changes in your replies to the Prelimenary Information forms between the time you supplied the information and before completion. If there have been any changes, i.e. the shed has fallen down or the central heating is not now working, you should notify your solicitor at once.

• **Transfer**

Your solicitor will in due course send you a transfer form for signature. This form shows the vendor(s) by name, the property, the purchase price and the name of the buyer(s), and will need to be signed by you in the presence of a witness and then returned to your solicitor.

• **Completion**

Completion should then take place on the date specified at exchange of contracts. This basically means that the deeds are transferred to the buyer in consideration of monies agreed as the purchase price. In most cases, the buyer and vendor contribute very little to the day of completion, but your solicitor should advise you that completion has taken place on the day, in order that you can safely relinquish possession of the property (and keys) to the new owner.

Solicitors acting for buyer and vendor do not physically meet in the bank lobby or office of lender or each other, and on behalf of their clients hand over documents in exchange for a cheque. Instead, and not nearly so dramatic, completion is provided for in the requisitions on the title in that the buyer gives undertakings, or there are implied undertakings, that he will pay over the money, and as soon as the money is received by the vendor's solicitor, he will in turn hold the documents which have been signed, sealed and properly executed to pay off any mortgage on that property, and then send these papers, usually by that night's post, to the solicitor acting for the purchaser. The buyer's solicitors do not then get the papers on the day of completion. In practical terms, what happens is that on the morning of completion the vendor's solicitor should be in receipt of the signed transfer. The purchaser's solicitor will telephone the vendor's solicitor and confirm that he has the funds and is now putting them in the telegraphic transfer (the bank transfer of money system). The vendor's solicitor will either accept that and release the keys (or give the vendor the okay to do so), or insist on waiting until the funds are actually received before releasing the keys. In this case, once confirmation is received from the bank (by phone usually) that the funds are received, the vendor's solicitor will then telephone the selling agent or vendor to say that keys can be released.

Leasehold properties

The legal process involved in selling leasehold properties follows much the same system as for freehold properties, but there are a few differences and complications which vendors should be aware of.

Firstly, the selling agents may need to see the lease before they produce written details and commence marketing. Potential buyers will naturally want to know details of the lease and any restrictions there may be, before making any offer or commitment to purchase. If there are unusual stipulations or conditions relating to your lease, you would do well to make sure your agents understand these fully in order that they can accurately relay explanations to potential purchasers and not mistakenly give vague information which could be misleading or off-putting.

Unfortunately, leases by nature are subject to complications, but assuming your solicitor approved the lease when you bought it, you should not experience any difficulty in transferring the lease to a new owner. Lenders are generally happy to fund the purchase of leasehold properties, so again, assuming your lease is sound, your buyer is unlikely to have trouble raising finance on it.

The vendor of a leasehold property will be required to supply his buyer's solicitor with details of the last three years' service charges to make sure these are not excessive, plus receipts for ground rent and a copy of the insurance policy and updated schedule. Because ground rents used to be nominal, often only £5 a year, many landlords did not bother to collect them. However, since technically it is the tenant's duty to pay the rent, and not the landlords duty to collect it, these rents are still liable to be paid at some point, giving the landlord the right of forfeiture. If you have not paid ground rent on the property you are selling, you will need to clarify any liability you have for back-payment.

DID YOU KNOW?   *Leasehold properties in Scotland are rare, and if found at all the leases usually run for several hundred years.*

DIY conveyancing

If you have common sense, a yen to save money and the temerity to question whether conveyancing can only be done by a solicitor or conveyancer, you may decide to do your own. Personally, I have yet to deal with a solicitor who did not do an excellent job on my behalf, and have always felt that the fee charged was well worth the cost, but you may feel differently.

For most people, the belief that solicitors are infallible is reason enough for enlisting their services, and most of us choose to relax in the knowledge that the conveyancing is being dealt with by people who know the system. However, solicitors can make mistakes and, more importantly, they are perhaps not as diligent as an interested party. This diligence is not so important for the seller but is vital when purchasing property, since relevant issues such as proposed buildings or new roads will only be uncovered by direct contact with the local council. A buyer will assume that his solicitor's mysterious 'searches' will uncover every possible issue relating to his new property, and hence won't bother to find out for himself, when in fact there may be some things which require further investigation or clarification.

Common practice implies that a solicitor is needed for conveyancing in much the same way that you need a dentist to remove a tooth. However, there is no law that says you can't remove your own teeth, and you are quite at liberty to handle the considerably less painful task of dealing with the administration relating to the sale of your own home.

BUT, and it is a big but, if you have no experience of dealing with authority, if you are not able to express yourself concisely, if you are daunted by official forms, if your buyer wants to proceed quickly, if you do not have plenty of spare time, if you are not prepared to read widely on the subject and lastly, if you hate paperwork, don't even consider it.

When the DIY conveyancer comes to handle redemption of his current mortgage, the mortgage company will almost certainly instruct their own solicitor, with whom the vendor will liaise and whose fee he will probably have to pay. There are also potential problems concerning deposits on exchange of contracts, in that very few solicitors acting for buyers will advise their clients to pay the deposit to a vendor in person (rather than to his solicitor if he was using one) as it could be spent, the vendor could be declared bankrupt, divorced or refuse to sell. The vendor will therefore not be in a position to use a deposit from the buyer as the deposit on his next purchase (if applicable), and so would need to find cash for the purpose.

A further point is that if the vendor is going on to purchase another property and is intending to handle the legal work relating to the purchase without a solicitor, he will almost certainly come up against opposition from his lender in that most mortgage companies will not process a loan application without details of the borrower's solicitor.

The financial picture

A conservative estimate for the cost of simultaneously selling one property and buying another can be put at around £5,000. Many of the costs will not be payable until monies resulting from the sale have been received, and these costs will then be deducted by the vendor's solicitor from the proceeds. However, some charges will require settlement before completion of the sale, like surveys and lender application fees, so these will need to be budgeted for. Solicitors sometimes require up to £100 from the vendor before commencing work to cover local search fees, because aborted sales are high and they are unwilling to personally pay for them if the sale falls through. It will seem that charges and fees result at every turn of the process moving home, and are likely to include:

- Solicitor's fees for the sale
- Solicitor's fees for the purchase (if applicable)
- Estate agency fees
- Lender's application and reservation fees
- Removal costs
- Surveyor's fees
- Local searches
- Land Registry fees
- Stamp Duty

DID YOU KNOW? *If you are taking out a new mortgage, you will normally have to pay the fee charged by your lender's solicitor for work he does on the lender's behalf.*

In payment for the estate agent's services, you will be sent an invoice showing the final sale figure, the agent's percentage commission of this figure, plus VAT on the fee at the current rate. You will not normally be expected to write out a cheque for this fee, and a copy of this invoice will usually be sent to your solicitor as well, so that the fee can be paid by your solicitor from the proceeds of the sale on completion.

Comet Estate Agents

To: Mr & Mrs Vendor
12 Lyndale Avenue
Stoke Lyndon
Warwickshire

Re: 12 Lyndale Avenue, Stoke Lyndon

To: Our Commission on the sale of the above property

Sale price achieved of £50,000.00	
Our scale: 2% of the sale price	1,000.00
VAT @ 17.5%	175.00
	———
Total due	1,175.00
	======

Having received a quote from your solicitor before instructing him, you will already know how much his fees will be. On completion, your solicitor will send you an invoice for his fees, but in practice this is only for your information. You will not normally be expected to furnish him with a cheque, since payment is usually be deducted directly from the sale proceeds. Check the invoice(s) carefully. If you are buying and selling simultaneously, you will be sent invoices covering both transactions, and these should obviously balance. See example opposite.

As you can see, the outstanding mortgage has been repaid (£30,000) and the cash needed to purchase the next property (£19,594.36) has been deducted, leaving a deficit payable by the client. In this example, therefore, a cheque for the deficit would be sent by the vendor to his solicitor, to enable him to complete the transaction. If there was an excess, the vendor would be sent a cheque. In this example, Mr & Mrs Vendor go on to purchase a subsequent property, so their solicitor has sent them an invoice outlining the purchase costs (see page 201.)

Had the purchase price in the example been in excess of £60,000, Mr & Mrs Vendor would have had the added expense of Stamp Duty to pay. Stamp Duty was introduced in 1981 and is a tax payable on the transfer of certain assets, including property valued in excess of £60,000. The rate of tax is currently 1% of the full value, not just the excess over £60,000.

RANDSFELL SOLICITORS

To: Mr & Mrs Vendor

INVOICE

SALE OF 12 LYNDALE AVENUE

Sale price		50,000.00
DEDUCT:		
Our professional charges	295.00	
VAT @ 17.5%	51.63	
PAID:		
Estate Agents	1,175.00	
Mortgage Redemption	30,000.00	
Office copies	14.00	
		31,535.63
		18,464.37
Less balance due to complete purchase		19,594.36
Balance due		£1,130.26
		=======

RANDSFELL SOLICITORS

To: Mr & Mrs Vendor

INVOICE

PURCHASE OF LAKE COTTAGE

Purchase price		54,000.00
ADD:		
Our professional charges	295.00	
VAT @ 17.5%	51.63	
PAID:		
Local search fee	56.00	
Official search fee	2.00	
Land Registry fees (not yet paid)	140.00	
Telegraphic Transfer fee	30.00	
	_____	574.63
		_____
		54,574.63
DEDUCT:		
Mortgage Advance	35,000.00	
Less Remittance fee	20.00	
	_____	(34,980.00)
		_____
Balance due to complete:		£19,594.63
		========

In summary:

- Vendor instructs solicitor and supplies him with any documentation which will be required upon securing a sale.
- Vendor advises lender and estate agent of name and address of solicitor.
- An acceptable offer is received.
- Vendor supplies solicitor with name and address of buyer and buyer's solicitor, and confirms purchase price.
- Survey / valuation carried out on behalf of buyer/lender.
- Buyer's solicitor puts searches in hand.
- Contracts are approved, signed and exchanged. Completion date agreed.
- Requisitions on title confirmed.
- Vendor signs and returns transfer documents to solicitor.
- Completion takes place.
- Solicitor redeems existing mortgage.
- Solicitor accounts to vendor for net proceeds of sale.

PROCEDURES IN SCOTLAND

Procedures for selling property in Scotland are in many ways different from the rest of the UK. The terminology used by solicitors and agents is not the same, so anyone used to buying and selling property in England will find the jargon relating to property transactions somewhat confusing in Scotland, and vice versa. In addition, the sequence of events and their timing, from viewing up to conclusion of the sale, is quite different.

DID YOU KNOW? *The timescale involved in the process of securing a property sale in Scotland is generally less than in England. The period between accepting an offer to the date of entry in Scotland is generally 4-5 weeks, whereas the time between acceptance of an offer and completion in England is commonly around 12 weeks.*

At the outset of a property sale in Scotland a purchaser makes a written offer through his solicitor which is binding if formally accepted. Both parties are then legally committed to conclude the deal, having thus entered into a binding contract. 'Missives' is the legal term referring to the formal correspondence which makes up the contract of the sale/purchase, which is usually drawn up by the solicitors acting on behalf of the purchaser and seller. Once missives have been concluded, the purchaser and seller are obligated to proceed with the transaction, and if either party is unable or unwilling to continue he or she will suffer a penalty of compensation for damages.

This is a surer system than that operating in England, where purchaser and seller are on tender hooks from the time a purchase price is agreed, right up to when contracts are exchanged. Until such time, the procedure remains 'subject to contract' (or subject to anything going wrong!), and each party is nervous that the other will have a change of heart and renege on the deal. If either party does pull out, for whatever reason, they are under no penalty for doing so, even though each party may by that time have incurred costs in legal fees, valuations, mortgage arrangement fees etc.

Date of entry

This is the date on which the purchaser can take possession of the property. The offer to purchase a property must include a date of entry. This enables the seller to know when he must vacate the property and gives him the opportunity to arrange removals and meter readings etc. in plenty of time. In England, the date of entry (or completion date) is not known until contracts are exchanged, and contracts may be exchanged only a few days before completion but many weeks (or even months) after the commencement of proceedings, which results in little notice for packing and removal arrangements.

Selling agents

Solicitors in Scotland have an added role to play in the purchase and sale of property, since they have traditionally acted as selling agents. So, as well as estate agents, sellers have the choice of promoting their property through the various solicitor–based marketing services, such as Solicitors' Property Centres, Solicitors' Estate Agencies and Solicitors' Property Registers.

The asking price

Once the estate agent has viewed the property, he and the seller will decide on a price which will reflect the value and attract purchasers. Sometimes agents will market a property at a specific price, but more often they ask for offers over a starting price which indicates the seller's base level, offers below which the seller will probably not accept. This encourages prospective purchasers to submit their best offer, because Each prospective purchasers know that if their offer is beaten they will not get the chance to submit a further (higher) one if someone else's is accepted.

In Scotland the purchaser's offer will normally represent the final selling price, whereas in England the original offer can be reduced by the purchaser, or rejected after initially being accepted by the seller, at any time before contracts are exchanged. When the property market in England was strong and there were several interested purchasers for every property, sellers would often raise the price part-way through proceedings or sell to a higher bidder in what came to be known as gazumping. Now that the property market has slumped, it is more common for the purchaser to reduce the price he is willing to pay part-way through proceedings, leaving the seller with little choice but to accept the lower offer if he is to continue with the sale.

DID YOU KNOW?   *In England the seller usually promotes the property at a price which is the maximum he can hope to achieve, accepting that potential purchasers will not offer the full amount. Such is the acceptance of price bargaining, that sellers often advertise an asking price which encourages purchasers to 'round down' the figure, i.e. they will advertise an asking price of £92,500 in anticipation of the purchaser knocking them down to a round £90,000.*

Closing dates

If a property attracts significant interest, indicating that more than one person would be prepared to submit an offer, the seller and his agents may set a deadline or closing date. This is a set time on a specific date by which all offers to be considered must be received. The prospective purchasers then submit their offers, knowing they are in competition with other purchasers, but not knowing the amount of the other offers. This goes some way to ensuring that prospective purchasers submit their best offer, by inference that they could be beaten by a higher bidder. The seller and his agents will then consider the offers received, but the seller is not obligated to accept the highest offer, or in fact any offer. He may decide to withdraw the property if none of the offers are satisfactory, because the offers he has received are probably the highest the property will achieve at that time. Alternatively, rather than removing the property from the market, the seller may continue to offer it for sale. However, the message to prospective purchasers who submit offers after the closing date is that the property did not reach it's anticipated price which is detrimental to the saleability of the property and the amount of any future offers.

When deciding to set a closing date, the seller should anticipate how much time the prospective purchasers who have shown an interest will need (to arrange mortgage funds and valuations or surveys) before setting the date. If prospective purchasers do not have sufficient time to prepare for submission of offers, they may be unable to meet the deadline of the closing date, and the seller may loose the chance of achieving a successful sale.

If the seller accepts an offer and instructs his solicitor to enter into negotiations with the successful purchaser, he cannot then accept a later offer from another party unless the original negotiations fall through.

This closing date system is extremely rare in England and will usually only be used when a property has been scheduled for sale by auction. If the property attracts sufficient interest prior to the auction date, the selling agent may decide that an acceptable offer could be reached without going to auction, and may encourage prospective purchasers to submit their offers in the hope of attracting not only those people who would have bid at auction, but also those who would have been unable or unwilling to do so.

Valuations and surveys

Valuations or surveys are carried out in Scotland before the prospective purchaser submits an offer, which may or may not be accepted by the seller. This can necessitate a prospective purchaser arranging (and paying for) several valuations or surveys before submitting a successful offer, but it does enable him to be in an informed position as to the condition of the property and its value before deciding how much it is worth to him and whether or not to proceed with the purchase. He is also assured that the property is a sound investment before committing himself to the purchase. After all, it would be disastrous to discover, once an offer has been accepted, that the property is falling down, because by that stage the commitment to buy has been made.

DID YOU KNOW?   *In England, it is usual for prospective purchasers to submit offers without first having obtained any information from a valuation or survey on which to base their opinion of the value.*

Chapter 9, Receiving an Offer, lists the various types of inspections a seller can expect to encounter from a prospective purchaser's surveyor.

The legal process

Between the time an offer is accepted and the property is officially owned by the purchaser, solicitors acting for purchaser and seller will have certain administrative duties to perform, including carrying out searches on the property, checking the title, and dealing with the transfer of ownership through preparing and executing the disposition. They will also need to comply with any legal formalities relating to funding arrangements (i.e. mortgage).

• Redeeming the mortgage

On accepting a formal offer, the seller knows that his purchaser will already have obtained mortgage funding if required. The seller's solicitor will now need to arrange for the existing mortgage on the property to be redeemed on receipt of monies from the purchaser in consideration of the purchase price. To do this, the solicitor will contact the seller's lender and obtain a statement showing the balance calculated to repay the loan, and this amount will be deducted by the solicitor on receipt of the purchase price. Anything left over is then given to the seller as a 'profit' from the sale.

• Buildings insurance

The seller should keep his buildings insurance in force until the purchaser takes possession of the property. If the insurance is arranged through the seller's lender, his solicitor will arrange for cancellation of the policy once the mortgage is repaid. If the seller has made personal buildings insurance arrangements he will need to arrange cancellation of the policy himself or ask his solicitor to do so, in which case his solicitor should be supplied with the policy details well in advance of the date of entry.

• Transferring ownership

Before the settlement date, the seller will be required to sign the disposition. This is the document which officially transfers ownership of the property from the seller to the purchaser. Once the sale price has been received by the seller's solicitor, this document will be delivered to the purchaser's solicitor.

• Settlement

Settlement of the transaction occurs when the purchaser's solicitor presents payment of the agreed price in exchange for the keys, the disposition and the title deeds. To cover the period of time it takes for the title to be registered, the seller's solicitor supplies a letter of obligation which protects the purchaser. Finally, the purchaser's solicitor must lodge the disposition transferring ownership and the standard security (the legal agreement that grants security over the property to the lender) with the relevant land register.

The purchase sum is usually received by the seller's solicitor in the form of a cheque which, while it is guaranteed, will probably take around four working days to clear through the banking system. This means that the seller's solicitor may not be in a position to pass the proceeds of the sale to the seller until the cheque has cleared.

In summary:

- The prospective purchaser contacts his solicitor with details of your property and registers his interest in buying it.
- The purchaser's solicitor registers his client's interest with the selling agents who advise the closing date for offers (if appropriate).
- Purchaser carries out survey on the property and arranges a mortgage.
- Purchaser submits an offer, which includes a date of entry, through his solicitor.
- If the offer is accepted, there is a binding contract.
- Purchaser's solicitor undertakes relevant searches, checks title etc.
- Seller's solicitor executes relevant documents and procedures to effect the transfer of ownership.
- Purchaser's solicitor delivers payment of the agreed selling price to the seller's solicitor.
- Seller's solicitor supplies keys to the property, the disposition transferring ownership and the title deeds.
- Title deeds are registered by the new owner.
- Purchaser's solicitor lodges the disposition and standard security with the relevant register.
- Seller's solicitor accounts to seller for net proceeds of sale.

MOVING OUT –
HEADACHES AND HEARTACHES

Moving home is exciting, rewarding and a chance for new beginnings. It also rates highly, alongside divorce and bereavement, for stress and has been the cause of many arguments and much disharmony. However, most of the stress involved in moving can be reduced with some advance planning, and by being aware of what is happening it is possible to avoid some of the nasty surprises which raise the blood pressure. By avoiding of last minute complications it might be possible to prevent a minor hiccup from becoming a major problem, and sort it out before it smacks you between the eyes. It would be impossible to prepare for every eventuality, and pondering too long on what might go wrong during a move is a sure way to give yourself a nervous breakdown. However it is necessary to embark upon some simple preparations if moving day has any hope of proceeding smoothly, and you will need to call on your reserves of patience to deal calmly with the inevitable upheaval.

Something which comes as a surprise to some people is that moving home is physically demanding. Even if a removals company has been hired to pack as well as transport furniture and effects, there will still be an element of packing to be done on the day, not to mention cleaning both the old and new home, keeping children occupied and supplying refreshments for yourself and removal men or helpers. Even for the well prepared, moving day is a tiring experience survived by good organisation and no small amount of luck; but for the hapless among us, chaos and confusion reigns. On the positive side, all the hard work and effort put into securing a sale and arranging the move has finally reached it's goal, which is reward in itself.

Advance preparations

Once contracts for the sale of the property have been exchanged (or in Scotland, once missives have been concluded), the date for completion will be determined. Under either system, vendors should discuss with their solicitor any preference regarding moving dates in advance, so that the arrangements are convenient to both parties. Throughout the sale they should keep in close contact with both the solicitor and selling agents, to make sure the sale is proceeding smoothly; that all relevant information has been obtained and dealt with in good time, and that they have done everything required of them.

Once the vendor is satisfied that the legal paperwork is on target for completion, he can begin the task of transferring services and advising those who need to know of the move, including:

- Insurance company
- Bank
- Milkman
- Vet
- DVLC – vehicle registration/driving licence (but remember you will need to produce your driving licence if hiring a van for the move).
- TV licence
- Rental/HP companies
- Doctor, dentist and optician
- Tax office
- Solicitor and other professional advisors
- Employer / work colleagues

In most cases a brief note is all that is needed, showing clearly your name, the address you are moving from, the address you are moving to and any reference number. Keep a copy of the letters so that you know who has been advised, or make a list of who you have written to and when, and keep that instead. Friends and family will also need to be advised which can involve many letters, so some people opt to have 'change of address' cards printed instead to save time.

As well as packing there will be several other jobs which are often so obvious that they get overlooked until the last minute. Some can be done well in advance and some will need to be left until the day before the move, but the less that needs attention on the day the better:

- Defrost fridge and/or freezer
- Dismantle as necessary, i.e. greenhouse, wardrobes
- Take down curtains and poles (if not included in the sale)
- Remove any fittings not included in the sale, i.e. light fittings
- Roll up rugs
- Return library books (if moving to a different area)
- Arrange disconnection of appliances

TOP TIP

Before moving day, make up a list of jobs which need to be done and check them off as you go along. This way you will not forget to collect the dry cleaning, arrange new pet tags, fill up with petrol or any of the other everyday things which tend to get overlooked in the furore.

Transferring services

• Telephone

British Telecom can transfer your existing telephone number to the new property (if the area code is the same) on the day of your move, and this is obviously very useful. In order for BT to arrange this service you must give at least two weeks notice by contacting the operator (on 150) and giving your details. If you are moving out of the area covered by your existing code, you will be given a new telephone number for your new address, or you can usually take over the one used by the present owners unless they are transferring it to their new address. Contact the operator, tell them your existing number and the address you are moving to. They will then dispatch the necessary forms for completion, and issue you with your new number. If your service is not from BT, but through an alternative system like Mercury, or if you use a pager or mobile phone, you will need to contact the relevant companies who supply the services, although most mobile phone users will naturally continue to use their existing number.

> **TOP TIP**
> If you know your new telephone number in advance, it can be included on your change of address cards.

• Council tax

When you know where you will be moving to, and when, contact the council to whom you presently pay Council Tax. Advise them of your current address, the date you will be vacating, and the address you are moving to. They will then calculate the relevant daily charge for the time you remain in your existing property and open a new account for your new property if it is within their governing area. If you are moving to a different part of the country, you will need to contact the local authority there.

• Electricity

The electricity company who supplies your power will need at least 2 working days' notice of your intended move. This is the minimum notice you are allowed to give by law, but ideally you should give at least a week. Write or telephone, giving your account number and the address of the property. If you are moving on a week day, the electricity company will arrange to read the meter on the day you move out. The account will then be closed and the final bill sent to your new address.

Similarly, an engineer will call at your new address (if this has been arranged) to take that reading, for which the previous owners will be billed, and a new account for the property will be opened in your name. If you are moving over the weekend, the process is much the same but instead of engineers taking the meter readings, you may need to make a note of readings yourself, at both the property you are vacating (before you leave), and the property you move to (on arrival). Write or phone your electricity company and let them know both readings so that they can arrange final billing for both accounts.

• Gas

If you need any appliances disconnected before you move, like the cooker, arrange an appointment in advance otherwise you may have to leave the appliance where it is until it can be disconnected, which will inconvenience both you and your buyer. The system of transferring the account and meter readings is much the same as for electricity (see above). If you use gas cylinders rather than mains gas, the cylinders are usually left behind for use by the new owner. The appliances will need careful disconnection and the cylinders should be turned off correctly so that they do not leak.

• Water

When you know the moving date, advise the company who supplies your water. Tell them your current address, the address you are moving to, and the date of the move. They will then prepare a final bill for your current address, calculating the daily charges to the last day of occupation. If you are moving within the same supply area, they will also open an account for your new address. If you are moving to a different supply area, contact the relevant company and advise the date from which you will be taking on the service. If you have a water meter this will need to be read, so contact the water company in the same way to arrange for them to call and take a reading. If the new property has a water meter, ask the water company to read the meter on the day you move in, or take the reading yourself on arrival.

• Post

Royal Mail operates a very useful service for mail re-direction. You may think you have advised everyone of your new address, but being sure all your mail will automatically be redirected should you have forgotten anyone, will give peace of mind. You can apply for redirection by completing the form supplied by the Royal Mail or by telephoning 0345-777888. Charges depend on the length of time redirection is arranged (1 month, 3 months or 1 year) and will be applied to each different surname, i.e. Mr & Mrs Jones will be charged one fee for both people, whereas Mr Green and Mr Smith will be charged twice.

Insurance

> **TOP TIP**
> Moving home may be the only time many people think of changing their insurance company. Some companies offer incentives to new customers which they do not broadcast to their existing clients, so it might be worth looking around for a better quote as a new customer rather than remaining with a company who may be taking your continued custom for granted.

Most removal and storage companies will arrange insurance policies to cover for loss or damage incurred during a move, but before going to the extra expense of taking out a policy with them, it is worth checking with your existing contents insurance company to see if you are already covered. If not, the company may be able to extend the policy to give adequate cover, although they will usually charge an additional premium. If you take out insurance through a removals company, check whether they are insuring all your goods or only those which they have packed, which is common practice. If 'owner packed' goods are excluded, this could leave many of your most precious possessions uninsured.

Insurance policies specifically concerned with removals frequently stipulate a time limit by which any claims must be submitted, after which they will not be accepted.

DID YOU KNOW? *Insurance cover offered by removal companies is not necessarily on a 'new for old' replacement basis, but rather a reimbursement based on market value.*

If you hire a van to do the move yourself, you will need to pay for insurance (probably arranged through the van hire company) to cover for loss or damage to the vehicle, and this insurance can carry a large excess figure (the part of any repair costs you will have to pay).

You may also find that moving into a new area affects your existing car insurance, since different areas attract different premium rates, depending on the perceived crime level in the locality.

Handing over the keys

Literally speaking, the vendor should leave a key to the property with his solicitor, who will hand it to the buyer once completion has taken place. In practice, most people leave a key with the estate agent who handled the sale, or alternatively with a neighbour. Naturally you will need to make sure the buyer knows where he can collect the key, otherwise you could be forced to wait until he arrives to hand them over personally, which will delay your own move. You need only supply a key to gain entry (usually the front door key), since all the others can be left inside the property, preferably labelled to show their usage.

If you make personal arrangements with the buyer regarding keys it is advisable to let your solicitor know your intention, but as a general rule keys should not be released without first checking with your solicitor that completion has taken place.

TOP TIP

Before packing away tools, compile an emergency tool kit to cope with any small jobs at the other end. Include string, a sharp knife, screwdriver, hammer, fuses and a torch.

Packing

If you are doing all the packing yourself, and not employing a removal company to do it for you, it is advisable to start the job of packing into boxes or crates at least two weeks before the moving date, because you can be fairly sure that it will take longer than anticipated. Rather than simply packing up each room in turn, it is useful to make a plan before you start so that non-essentials are packed first, which also makes the unpacking easier at the other end since you will know which boxes can be unpacked at your leisure and which will need to be unpacked fairly quickly.

By labelling boxes by room (i.e. 'Johnny's room', 'study' etc.), you can unload each box directly into its correct room and avoid wasting time and energy moving boxes from room to room instead of putting them in the right place to begin with. The simplest way to orchestrate packing with unpacking is to draw up a floor plan of your new home, marking each room with a code, so that boxes marked with a green sticker will be unloaded straight into the room shown on the plan with a green sticker.

> **TOP TIP**
> To see what kitchen equipment can be packed in advance and
> what needs to be available until the last minute, prepare an
> average day's meals, but don't put anything you use back in the
> cupboards. This pile of pans, crockery and cutlery left out will be
> what you use regularly; the rest can be packed away.

Some people like to sort through and pile up their possessions
before actually packing them into boxes, while others prefer to go
straight from shelf to box. Either way you will need plenty of boxes or
crates; double what you think you will use. Some removal firms
supply boxes, but they often have to be emptied on arrival at the
delivery address so that the driver can take them back to the depot, or
else a rental charge is made. If you don't have boxes supplied by a
removal firm, you could ask your local supermarket for some of the
boxes their deliveries arrive in. Care should naturally be taken to
ensure that boxes containing fragile items are marked accordingly so
that they are not piled underneath anything heavy, and that the 'right
way up' is clearly displayed. Some sort of padding will also be needed
to wrap around fragile items, so ask neighbours or friends to save
their newspapers for you.

Always label boxes to show their contents, even if only to identify
the rooms from which they came. You may think you will remember
what you put in each, but as more and more are filled and sealed, the
job of finding a single item becomes like looking for a needle in a
haystack, and of course if you do need to find something it will
probably be in the last box you look in.

It is a good idea to mark one box 'Do Not Remove' and put into
this anything you do not want to go in the removal van, including for
example:

- Kettle and tea things (a carton of UHT milk can be packed in advance since it does not require refrigeration until opened)
- Light bulbs / candles / torch
- Toilet roll, soap and a towel
- Cleaning materials
- Small amount of cash
- Children's favourite toys
- Dog's favourite bone
- Any paperwork concerning the purchase/sale just in case there is a problem.

It might also be useful to transport a vacuum cleaner separately so that the carpets at the new address can be cleaned before being covered up by furniture when the removals van arrives and starts unloading.

DID YOU KNOW?   *Freezers and fridges must be transported upright and should be left to stand in their new position for at least 2 hours before being switched on again (refer to manufacturer's handbook).*

If a removal firm is packing for you, they may come the day before the move to pack, then return on the day to load up. This is because they appreciate that the moving day is not the time to be frantically filling boxes and crates, and as far as possible everything should be packed before. There will be some last minute bits and pieces to pack; items which need to be used until the last minute (bedding, toiletries etc.), and these will take enough time without adding to them.

When the van arrives, it makes sense to arrange the loading so that those things which will be needed first at the other end go into the van last. For example:

- Carpet / rugs
- Beds and bedding
- Wardrobes

- Appliances like cooker or fridge
- Children's bedroom contents (get them occupied as soon as possible)

If you are using a removal firm and not travelling in the van yourself, you will need to transport your family, pets, and whatever you do not want to go in the van. If you do not have a car, it might be worth borrowing or even hiring one for the day, or making arrangements for taxi hire.

Removals

Hiring a professional removal firm can be expensive, and whether or not you choose this option, as opposed to hiring a van and doing it yourself, will depend on the distance involved, how fit you are, how much furniture you have to move and whether much of it is heavy or awkward to shift.

DID YOU KNOW? *Unless you hold an HGV (heavy goods vehicle) driving licence, the size of van you are permitted to hire will be no more than 7 1/2 tonnes laden weight.*

Although DIY moving is cheaper, the disadvantages should not be overlooked and can far outweigh the saving:

- Loading and unloading will take longer since you are unlikely to be as experienced as the removal staff.
- You will probably need to make more than one journey because the size of van will be too small to take everything in one go, and you will not be experienced enough to make the full use of the space available.
- You are more likely to suffer damage to goods because you will not be adept at loading and handling. Removal men may appear to

220

take less care with handling than you would yourself, but their experience enables them to know how best to avoid damage.

- It is physically strenuous – washing machines and wardrobes are even heavier than they look.
- It is emotionally more exhausting because you have more to think about.
- Negotiating stairs etc. with heavy goods may require lifting gear which you will not have.
- Any problems which need dealing with at the last minute will cause delays if you are preoccupied with loading and unloading.

If you decide to use a removal firm, it is worth getting several quotes before making a choice. The choice of firm need not be limited to those in the area you are moving from, so you could consider using a firm in the area you are moving to, since the travelling for them is just the same. This can be worthwhile if moving from, say, London to Cornwall when the London based companies are likely to charge more than the Cornish companies.

TOP TIP

If you hire a van to move a long distance, bear in mind that you will probably have to bring it back to where you hired it from, giving yourself extra travelling.

An assessor from the removal firms will normally come to the property to asses the amount of furniture and effects to be moved before giving a quote. Be sure to disclose everything (including the contents of loft, garage, garden shed), otherwise you may find the van they send is too small. If the move is likely to involve special requirements (maybe because access for the van at the other end is difficult or there are a lot of stairs for the removal men to negotiate), mention this to the assessor since he will need to consider all aspects of the move before submitting a quote. On acceptance of a quote, it is worthwhile to confirm in writing any special requirements you have discussed, so that there is no argument later about these being allowed for in the quote.

The amount of notice needed to book a removal firm varies: some only need a week, whereas others ask for a month. Friday and Saturday are the most popular days for moving, and the end of the month is always busy, so try to avoid these if you can. Also, if on arrival at your new home, you need the emergency services of a plumber or electrician, they may not be available over the weekend, and if they are, their fee will be higher than during the week.

Payment will usually be requested in advance, but some firms accept payment on the day. If you pay in cash, make sure you get a receipt from the driver. You may decide to give the removal men a tip, but this is not compulsory, and certainly if you have any cause for complaint you should not do so, since a tip will be construed as an indication of complete satisfaction on your part, and any later complaint or claim for damage could be viewed with suspicion.

The removal men often plan to arrive early on the morning of the move. To load the contents of an average 3 bed house or flat takes around three hours, so they aim to be loaded up by noon, in time for the arrival of the new owners and their removal van. By the time you arrive at your new home, the previous owners will, with any luck, be on their way to their new home, and so on.

Once everything has been loaded, but before the removal van departs, take a careful look around to make sure nothing has been forgotten. Sometimes the most obvious things get left behind (like a picture or rug) because we are so accustomed to seeing them in their position that they do not stand out. Also, things which are kept out of sight for most of the time, like the contents of the garage or loft can be overlooked.

Turn off the heating (if that is what you have arranged with the new owners), make sure all the windows are closed and the entrance doors are locked, and take any necessary meter readings for connected services like gas and electricity. If you are using removal men, make sure they have the correct address of your new home, giving directions as necessary. They will probably take longer than you to arrive, giving you time to have a cup of tea and something to eat before starting the unloading and unpacking.

If you are not moving any great distance, unloading will probably be completed during the afternoon. If you are moving far, the removal company may unload the day after loading, so you will need to arrange overnight accommodation unless you are happy to spend the first night in your new home without any furniture. This will need to be discussed with the removal company when their services are booked.

Storage

For vendors involved in a staggered move, maybe selling their home and moving into furnished rented accommodation temporarily before purchasing again, it might be necessary to put some or all of the furniture and possessions into storage. Many removal companies, especially the larger ones, offer storage facilities and the loading and unloading procedure is much the same as with a normal move, but with a gap in-between of however long the storage is used. The removal men will arrive to load up in the usual way and will then take the cargo to the storage site. Stored goods used to be held in warehouses, but nowadays containers are generally used. The goods are transferred from your home into sealed containers which remain unopened until they are delivered to the final destination. This reduces the chance of loss or damage and also cuts down on dust and dirt.

DID YOU KNOW? *Some storage companies offer rental of secure individual units, which have unlimited access by the hirer, who has a key and can come and go at his leisure.*

You can store virtually everything, except plants, perishable goods, and anything flammable. No special packing is usually needed to protect goods during a short storage period, although carpets or rugs should ideally be cleaned beforehand and clothes treated against moths.

Deciding which possessions to store needs careful thought:

- You do not want to omit anything which it later transpires should have been stored, so it is useful to make a comprehensive list of items which are supplied at your temporary accommodation (like bedding or kitchen equipment), so that you know exactly what would be superfluous to bring yourself. If you decide in retrospect that some items need to be added to your container, the storage company will usually arrange this, as long as you deliver them to the storage site yourself. If you ask them nicely and do not make a habit of it, they might not even make a charge, but check first.

- The opposite (and more common) problem occurs when some items have been put into storage which it soon transpires should not have been. Should any items need to be retrieved before the goods are delivered en mass, the storage company will almost certainly charge a fee, and will probably need advance notice so that they can open the container at their convenience. If you know you are likely to need some items sooner than the rest, speak to the storage company in advance and they will advise whether or not they can store specific items separately so that they are available for collection. If they deliver them, there will be a charge.

If you are planning to use storage facilities, this could double the cost of the move because everything is moved twice; once from the property into storage containers, then out of storage to the final destination. Storage charges are usually made per container, per week, and as a general guide an average three bed house or flat will need around 3 containers.

The storage company will probably prepare their own inventory listing items of furniture, but the contents of cartons may not be specific, saying only 'carton of books' or 'carton of china'. It is useful to prepare a comprehensive inventory yourself, and it will be helpful when you unpack if the inventory identifies what is packed into each carton, showing for example that carton No.1 contains kitchen equipment so that this carton can be unloaded directly into the kitchen and not hidden under several other cartons in another room. As with normal removals, 'owner packed' goods are not usually covered by the storage company's insurance for breakage, and the insurance generally may not be on a 'new for old' replacement basis. Your own insurance company might be able to offer better cover, so check with them first.

Unpacking

Having prepared the process for moving your goods out, you now have to arrange the smooth moving in. On arrival at your new home, before the removal van arrives, take a good look round the property to make sure everything which should have been left has been, and if there are any omissions speak to your solicitor. If the central heating has been turned off, you might like to get this running, but in any event check that the heating and other appliances are working. If you have arranged for connection of appliances and meter readings you can expect a stream of callers, but if you have not arranged for meter readings to be taken by the suppliers concerned make a note of the readings yourself and put them in a safe place.

Assuming you arranged for a telephone service to be supplied, the telephone should be working, but if on arrival you are faced with a dead line it will be necessary to contact the operator (from a public phone box) to prompt connection at the exchange.

When the removal van arrives, don't automatically start unpacking the first box which comes off it, even though you will have loaded in some kind of order at the other end. Instead, have a plan of what to deal with in order of importance, so that you are not worn out by unpacking incidentals, before you get round to unpacking the things you need immediately. The order of unpacking will depend on personal priorities. Some people like to hang up their clothes before hanging the curtains; some like to get the kitchen organised first, whilst for others the priority is sorting out the living room. However, most people agree that it is very tedious to find yourself hunting for sheets and bedding late in the evening when you are tired, especially if there are children who are equally worn out, so it is advisable to put bed making at the top of the list.

If the property was furnished and occupied when you viewed it prior to moving in, it will look quite different when empty. You may even be dismayed to find that the room sizes seem different to how you remembered them, or that electric sockets are not suitably positioned, making your planned furniture arrangement unworkable. If this is the case, trying different arrangements immediately on arrival will only lead to irritation and despondency. Instead it is better to give the arrangement some thought overnight and then tackle it with a fresh eye the following day.

Preparing children

The age of your children are will probably determine the amount of involvement they have in the move, and whether they are there on the day at all. Very young children might be best left with grandparents or friends, especially if you are likely to find the ordeal stressful and relay that feeling to the child. When collecting them, bear in mind that they will be very disorientated so try to allow time for them to explore and settle in before bedtime. If the children are old enough to particpate in the move they will want to get their bearings on arrival at the new home. Once they have satisfied their curiosity, they could be kept busy with drawing or a puzzle in a quiet spot where they can't get into any mischief and won't get under your feet. Letting a child select a favourite toy to bring with them, rather than hunting for something suitable amongst packed boxes when you arrive, will reduce the chance of tantrums.

Older children generally like to be involved and will probably enjoy arranging their own bedroom. If possible it is helpful for them to see their new home in advance of the move, so that they know what to expect.

When to tell children about a move will depend on the individual child and how you think they will react to the news. Young children will not understand why they are moving and can become quite distressed to know in advance of an impending change. If they are upset by the idea, tell them all the positive aspects of the move, like a park or swimming pool nearby, so that they have something positive to look forward to. Older children should really be told about the move early on in proceedings, especially if they will need to change schools since joining a different school as 'the new kid' is a frightening prospect and will take some getting used to. If told early on, this also safeguards against the possibility of them finding out by accident from someone else.

As regards schooling, if the move necessitates a change of school you will need to contact the local authority covering the area you are moving to, asking them to send information about the schools in that area. You will also need to write to the head teacher at the child's current school to advise when he or she will be leaving.

With children of all ages, it is useful to ask the existing occupiers of your new home if there are any children of a similar age nearby, so that your offspring can make new friends immediately.

Pampered pets

Pets have no understanding of what is happening to their home when it gets turned upside down on moving day, so making an extra fuss of them will help to allay their fears and confusion. Naturally it is essential to make sure pets have water available at all times and it will be a good idea to have at least enough food for the first few days in the new home to tide them over until you have time and energy to go shopping again.

For pets who have identity chip implants it will be necessary to advise the company who hold the register of the change of address.

Cats

Cats have a habit of going AWOL just as the last items are placed in the removal van, so keeping them safely inside will avoid wasting time calling for Tiddles until he deigns to return. Cats do not travel well loose in the car and are a hazard for the driver, so it is preferable to transport them in a suitable container with plenty of ventilation.

On arrival at your destination, cats should be kept inside until they are settled or else you may find, being territorial animals, that they are unsettled enough to go back 'home'. The length of time a cat needs to be kept inside will depend to some extent on whether he has moved before and the personality of the individual, but most cats will need at least a few days to settle in before confronting their new area. When letting a cat out for the first few times, if this is done before feeding time there is something good for him to come back for.

Have plenty of cat litter and a suitable tray for the period of confinement, and remember to change the address on the identity tag.

Dogs

Dogs are best kept in the garden whilst the loading is under way, assuming it is escape proof. If a dog is nervous or apt to guard, he will find the presence of removal men something of a worry, and will be far happier away from the proceedings.

When transporting a dog to your new home by car, allow him plenty of ventilation. If travelling a long distance the dog will benefit from regular stops to spend a penny, but it might not be advisable, given the strange surroundings and upset of the move, to let him off the lead.

DID YOU KNOW? *Dogs can die in cars very quickly on a warm day, even if the sun is not shining. They can also suffer heat stroke in a moving car, even in cold weather, when the sun shines on them through a hatchback window.*

On arrival at the new home, check fences and boundaries are secure enough to prevent escape if you intend putting a dog in the garden, especially if he is to be left unattended. Put the dog's bed, toys, feeding and water bowls in a suitable place, so that at least something is normal and he can identify the strange new place as his home. If you have rules about which areas of the home your dog has access to, you should establish these as soon as possible to avoid confusion.

Other animals
Small animals such as gerbils and hamsters should be contained in their cage or a suitable box (one which they cannot chew through) and transported with you, not in the removals van amongst other boxes and crates. For fish, birds and exotic pets, consult your vet or supplier for specialist advice.

In summary:
- Be aware of potential problems before they surprise you.
- Circulate change of address details and arrange transfer of services well in advance.
- Give some thought to the unpacking and how you will tackle this, before embarking on the packing.

- Consider the pros and cons of either employing a removal firm or hiring a van for a DIY move, before deciding which option to take.
- Make sure you have adequate insurance.